rice

rice

Great recipe ideas with a classic ingredient

>> in 60 ways

Marshall Cavendish
Cuisine

The publisher wishes to thank **Lim's Arts and Living** for the loan and use of their tableware.

Design: Agnes Lim
Photography: Jambu Studio

Other Marshall Cavendish Offices:
Marshall Cavendish Ltd. 119 Wardour Street, London W1F 0UW, UK • Marshall Cavendish Corporation. 99 White Plains Road, Tarrytown NY 10591-9001, USA • Marshall Cavendish International (Thailand) Co Ltd. 253 Asoke, 12th Flr, Sukhumvit 21 Road, Klongtoey Nua, Wattana, Bangkok 10110, Thailand • Marshall Cavendish (Malaysia) Sdn Bhd, Times Subang, Lot 46, Subang Hi-Tech Industrial Park, Batu Tiga, 40000 Shah Alam, Selangor Darul Ehsan, Malaysia

Marshall Cavendish is a trademark of Times Publishing Limited

National Library Board Singapore Cataloguing in Publication Data

Rice in 60 ways : great recipe ideas with a classic ingredient. – Singapore : Marshall Cavendish Cuisine, 2006.
p. cm. – (In 60 ways)
ISBN-13 : 978-981-261-2335
ISBN-10 : 981-261-233-5

1. Cookery (Rice) I. Title: Rice in sixty ways II. Series: In 60 ways

TX809.R5
641.6318 -- dc21   SLS2006006963

Printed in Singapore by Times Graphics Pte Ltd

contents >>

introduction »

Rice is a rich source of complex carbohydrates, or starch. Simple carbohydrates are also known as sugars. Although both types become sugars upon breaking down in the body, complex carbohydrates take more time to digest than their simple counterparts and, as a result, keep a person feeling full for longer. The nutritional profile of rice is made more attractive by the fact that it also contains only trace amounts of fat and sodium and no cholesterol or gluten. Rice is relatively low in protein, but because it is often eaten with soy products in the East, the deficiency is overcome.

The earliest known historical records indicate that the Chinese were the first in the world to cultivate rice some 4,000 years ago. The Chinese later introduced the processes to India, and the cultivation of rice began to flourish far and wide in Asia. Today, rice is grown around the world—in Asia, Australia, Africa, Latin America, parts of Europe and the United States. Asia, however, remains the largest cultivator and consumer of rice, at 90 per cent of world production.

Varieties of Rice: the Long and Short of it

Within the single species of rice (oryza sativa), there are thousands of varieties. Only a few hundred are cultivated throughout the world, however, and the most common classifications to consumers are the length and colour of the grain.

Long-grain rice has long, slender kernels and when cooked, the grains remain separate and are light and fluffy. Long-grain rice comes in two main types: white and brown. Brown rice is more nutritious than its white counterpart because of its outer coating, the bran layer. Rice bran contains proteins and minerals, and is rich in dietary fibre. White rice grains, or polished rice, have had both their husks and bran layers removed through milling. As a result, white rice grains predominantly contain complex carbohydrates. The two most common types of long-grain rice are jasmine rice and basmati rice. Jasmine rice is also known as Thai fragrant rice for the aroma that it gives off when cooked. It is commonly used in Asian recipes. Basmati rice is also extremely aromatic, but its fragrance is distinctively earthy and nuttier. It is commonly used in Indian and Middle Eastern recipes.

Short-grain rice is generally starchier than long-grain varieties. When cooked, the grains tend to cling together. Varieties of short-grain rice include Arborio, Japanese and glutinous rice. Arborio rice is ideal for risottos because the grains are able to absorb large amounts of liquid during cooking to develop a creamy texture without becoming mushy. Japanese rice is also known as sushi rice and the grains become sticky when cooked, a quality similar to white glutinous rice. White glutinous rice is commonly used in a variety of sweet and savoury Asian recipes. Black glutinous rice is popularly used in desserts. It has a chewy texture and nutty flavour and turns a deep purple colour with cooking.

Wild rice (Zizania aquatica), known to some as Canadian/Indian rice or water oats, comes from an aquatic plant that belongs to the same generic family of grass (Graminae) as common rice (oryza sativa), but is ultimately a different species altogether.

Wild rice takes nearly twice as long to cook but its great chewy texture is well worth the wait. Wild rice is also far less starchy and very flavourful.

Storage

If kept in an airtight container in a cool, dark place, rice will keep for up to a year. Brown rice will last between three and six months in the same conditions. This is because the bran layer is more prone to spoiling. When storing cooked rice, leave to cool thoroughly before transferring to a covered container and keep refrigerated. Cooked rice can keep for up to 1 week in the refrigerator, or for several months in the freezer.

Cooking

Rice grains generally increase 2½ to 3 times in volume when cooked. To cook rice successfully, always follow the manufacturer's instructions and measure water and rice accurately. Rice can be cooked by boiling or steaming, and on the stove, in the microwave oven or using an electric rice cooker. When rice is cooked, allow it to stand for 5–10 minutes, covered, so the cooking process can be completed with the residual heat and the moisture from the steam can be fully absorbed by the rice to become tender and fluffy.

vegetarian

avgolemono
(greek egg and lemon soup)

An unusual soup with the refreshing flavours of lemon juice and parsley, this dish is light enough for even the hottest summer's day.

Serves 6

Ingredients

Long-grain rice	90 g (3 oz)
Vegetable or chicken stock	1.9 litres (3 pints / 7½ cups)
Eggs	4
Lemon juice	squeezed from 2 lemons
Freshly ground black pepper	to taste
Salt	to taste
Parsley	2 sprigs, chopped

Method

- Wash rice thoroughly, then soak in cold water for 30 minutes and drain before use.
- Bring stock to the boil in a large saucepan. Add rice and simmer over low heat for 15 minutes or until rice is tender. Remove from heat.
- Break eggs into a mixing bowl and beat well with a whisk.
- Gradually add lemon juice, beating continuously. Add a few spoonfuls of stock, a little at a time, beating constantly until it is well mixed.
- Stir egg mixture into rice until well mixed, then place over moderate heat for 2–3 minutes. Do not bring to the boil or soup will curdle.
- Season to taste, sprinkle parsley over and serve immediately.

chinese-style vegetable fried rice

A great way to use up leftover rice, this dish uses common store-cupboard items and is quick to prepare.

Serves 2

Ingredients

Cooking oil	2 Tbsp
Garlic	1 clove, peeled and chopped
Cooked long-grain rice	300 g (10½ oz), cold
Carrots	80 g (3 oz), peeled, diced and blanched
Frozen green peas	80 g (3 oz), blanched
Frozen sweet corn kernels	80 g (3 oz), blanched
Light soy sauce	1 tsp or to taste
Ground white pepper	1 tsp or to taste
Red chilli	1, seeded if desired and sliced
Spring onion (scallion)	1, chopped

Method

- Heat oil in a wok and stir-fry garlic until lightly browned and fragrant. Add rice and toss briefly to break up any lumps.

- Mix in carrots, peas and corn. Season to taste with soy sauce and pepper. Stir-fry for 2–3 minutes.

- Sprinkle in chilli and spring onion. Toss a few times to mix, then dish out. Serve hot.

thai pineapple rice

A classic Thai dish, its tangy flavour makes a great foil for most coconut milk-based curries. To make this dish vegetarian, omit dried prawns and replace fish sauce with a soy-based seafood marinade.

Serves 4

Ingredients

Pineapple	1, medium
Cooking oil	3 Tbsp
Dried prawns (shrimps) (optional)	90 g (3 oz), rinsed and drained
Chopped garlic	3 Tbsp
Cooked Jasmine rice	800 g (1¾ lb), thoroughly cooled
Fish sauce	3 Tbsp or to taste
Sugar	1 Tbsp or to taste
Chilli powder (optional)	1 tsp or to taste

Garnishing

Crisp-fried shallots

Roasted cashews

Coriander leaves (cilantro)

Sliced red chillies

Pork or chicken floss (optional)

Method

- Peel, core and remove eyes from pineapple, then chop into small cubes. Alternatively, halve unpeeled pineapple lengthways and run a sharp knife about 2-cm (1-in) from the edge all around, then scoop out pineapple flesh. Reserve pineapple shells for serving later.

- Heat oil in a wok or large pan. Fry dried prawns, if using, until fragrant, then dish out and set aside.

- In the same oil, fry garlic until lightly brown and fragrant. Add rice and stir-fry, breaking up lumps. Season with fish sauce, sugar and chilli powder, if using.

- Add pineapple cubes and fried prawns, if using. Stir until ingredients are well mixed and rice is dry after absorbing juices from pineapple cubes. Adjust seasoning to taste.

- Dish out to a serving platter, individual serving plates or pineapple shells. Garnish as desired and serve hot.

nasi kunyit
(malay turmeric rice)

This dish makes an attractive and flavourful alternative to plain steamed rice, and goes well with chicken or beef curries.

Serves 6

Ingredients

Turmeric	5-cm (2-in) knob
Uncooked glutinous rice	450 g (1 lb)
Water	
Screwpine (*pandan*) leaves	2–3, washed and knotted
Coconut milk	150 ml (5 fl oz), mixed with ½ tsp salt

Method

- Peel and clean turmeric, then pound until fine using a mortar and pestle.
- Extract turmeric juice by passing through a fine sieve or squeezing with a piece of muslin cloth.
- Put rice into a bowl and add turmeric juice. Add enough water to cover rice. Leave to soak for at least 3 hours or preferably overnight.
- Drain rice and transfer to a heatproof (flameproof) dish. Top with screwpine leaves and steam for 30 minutes.
- Remove rice from steamer and discard screwpine leaves. Stir in coconut milk, then return to steamer for 10 minutes.
- Serve rice with chicken or beef curries.

one-dish turmeric rice

An adaptation of the traditional dish using common store-cupboard items, this dish can be served as it is, or with fried chicken or fish for a heartier meal.

Serves 6

Ingredients

Vegetable oil	3 Tbsp
Onion	1, large, peeled and finely chopped
Garlic	2 cloves, peeled and crushed
Ground turmeric	1 Tbsp
Salt	1 tsp or to taste
Freshly ground black pepper	1 tsp or to taste
Finely chopped lemon grass	1 tsp, or ½ tsp finely grated lemon rind
Long-grain rice	450 g (1 lb), washed, soaked in cold water for 30 minutes and drained
Water	625 ml (1 pint / 2½ cups)
Coconut milk	300 ml (10 fl oz)
Bay leaves	2, fresh or dried

Garnishing

Eggs	3, hard-boiled, shelled and sliced
Peanuts	120 g (4 oz / 1 cup), roasted and coarsely chopped
Crisp-fried shallots	4 Tbsp
Coriander leaves (cilantro)	4 sprigs
Bananas	2, peeled and sliced

Method

- Heat oil in a large, heavy saucepan over moderate heat. Fry onion and garlic, stirring occasionally, for 5–7 minutes or until onion is soft and translucent but not brown.

- Stir in turmeric, seasoning, lemon grass and rice. Fry for a further 5 minutes, stirring constantly.

- Add water and coconut milk, increase heat to high and bring to the boil.

- Reduce heat to low, add bay leaves and cover pan. Simmer rice for 15–20 minutes or until all the liquid has been absorbed and rice is light and fluffy.

- Remove from heat and discard bay leaves. Dish out to a serving platter or individual serving plates.

- If using a platter, shape rice into a dome. Garnish as desired and serve immediately.

- Alternatively, serve garnishing ingredients on the side and allow diners to help themselves.

japanese mushroom soup with brown rice

Quick and easy to prepare, this makes a great one-dish meal, especially after a long day at work.

Serves 2–3

Ingredients

Dashi	1 litre (32 fl oz / 4 cups)
Salt	1 tsp or to taste
Japanese light soy sauce	3 Tbsp or to taste
Fresh shiitake mushrooms	100 g (3½ oz), thinly sliced
Chinese chives	1 sprig, cut into 2.5-cm (1-in) lengths
Eggs	2, beaten
Cooked brown rice	500 g (1 lb 1½ oz)

Method

- Combine dashi stock, salt and soy sauce in a pot. Bring to the boil.

- Reduce heat, add mushrooms and simmer for 5 minutes or until mushrooms are cooked.

- Add chives and adjust seasoning to taste. Add eggs in a slow steady stream to form egg ribbons. Remove from heat.

- Divide brown rice among individual serving bowls. Shape rice in each bowl into a mound, if desired.

- Ladle soup over and serve. If serving rice in a mound, add soup slowly around the mound so that it keeps its shape.

Ready-made dashi is available at most supermarkets or Asian stores. Dashi powder, paste or concentrate are also handy.

khichri
(indian rice with lentils)

This is a lightly aromatic mixture of rice and lentils from India and the dish from which the English evolved Kedgeree. Serve it with spiced vegetables.

Serves 4

Ingredients

Long-grain rice	240 g (8 oz), washed and drained
Moong dhal or yellow lentils	120 g (4 oz), washed and drained
Butter	5 Tbsp
Onion	1, peeled and finely chopped
Ginger	2.5-cm (1-in) knob, peeled and finely chopped
Garlic	1 cloves, peeled and finely chopped
Black peppercorns	6
Bay leaf	1
Salt	1 tsp
Ground turmeric	½ tsp
Boiling hot water	625 ml (1 pint / 2½ cups)

Garnishing

Crisp-fried shallots
Mint leaves

Method

- Combine rice and dhal or lentils in a large bowl. Add enough water to cover and leave to soak for 1 hour. Drain before use.
- Melt 3 Tbsp butter in a large saucepan over moderate heat. When foam subsides, add onion and fry for 4 minutes, stirring occasionally.
- Add ginger, garlic, peppercorns and bay leaf. Fry for another 4 minutes or until onion is golden brown.
- Add rice, dhal, salt and turmeric. Stir and toss mixture gently. Reduce heat to moderate–low and cook for 5 minutes, stirring gently.
- Add hot water and stir once, then cover pan and reduce heat to low. Cook for 15–20 minutes or until rice and dhal are cooked and all the water has been absorbed.
- Stir in remaining butter with a fork and remove from heat. Transfer to a serving dish, garnish as desired and serve.

Moong dhal is the Indian name for mung or green beans that have been skinned and split.

italian green rice

This delicious and very attractive Italian dish with layers of rice, peas and spinach makes an interesting supper dish.

Serves 4–6

Ingredients

Water	650 ml (21½ fl oz)
Salt	3 tsp
Italian rice	180 g (6 oz), use Arborio or similar
Fresh green peas	450 g (1 lb), removed from pods
Spinach	900 g (2 lb)
Freshly ground black pepper	1 tsp
Butter	3 Tbsp
Chopped basil	1 tsp
Chopped marjoram	1 tsp
Parmesan cheese	30 g (1 oz), grated

Method

- Combine 450 ml (15 fl oz) water and 1 tsp salt in a large saucepan. Bring to the boil over high heat.

- Add rice and stir well. Cover pan, reduce heat to moderate and simmer for 15–20 minutes or until rice is tender and fluffy.

- Meanwhile, combine peas, remaining water and 1 tsp salt in a medium saucepan. Cook over moderate heat for 8 minutes or until tender. Drain peas in a colander and set aside.

- Wash spinach well and transfer to another medium saucepan; do not drain. Add remaining salt, place over moderate heat and cook for 7–12 minutes or until just tender. Do not add any water because there is enough left after washing.

- Drain spinach in a colander, pressing down with a wooden spoon to extract any excess liquid.

- Chop spinach and sprinkle with pepper. Spread one-third over base of a shallow heatproof (flameproof) dish.

- When rice is cooked, add 2 Tbsp butter, basil and marjoram. Toss until rice is well coated, then spread one-third over spinach.

- Purée peas in a blender (processor) or mash them through a strainer, then spread one-third over rice.

- Repeat layers with remaining thirds until ingredients are used up.

- Preheat grill (broiler) to high. Meanwhile, sprinkle cheese over top layer, then dot with remaining butter that has been cut into small cubes.

- Place dish under grill for 3–4 minutes or until cheese is melted and lightly browned. Serve immediately.

indian rice with aubergine and potatoes

Inspired by a recipe from the west coast of India, this dish may be served with raita, chutneys and pappadum for an economical meal.

Serves 4

Ingredients

Long-grain rice	300 g (10 oz), washed, soaked in cold water for 30 minutes and drained
Water	625 ml (1 pint / 2½ cups)
Salt	1 tsp
Ghee (clarified butter)	60 g (2 oz / ¼ cup)
Potatoes	360 g (12 oz), peeled and cut into 2.5-cm (½-in) cubes
Aubergine (eggplant)	1, large, cubed and degorged
Butter	60 g (2 oz), melted

Spice paste

Ground turmeric	1 tsp
Ground cumin seeds	1 tsp
Ground coriander seeds	1 Tbsp
Cayenne pepper	½ tsp
Sugar	½ tsp
Salt	½ tsp
Chickpea flour	2 tsp
Lemon juice	1 Tbsp

Method

- Combine rice, water and salt in a large saucepan. Bring to the boil over high heat.

- Cover saucepan, reduce heat to very low and simmer for 15–20 minutes or until rice is tender and all the water has been absorbed. Remove from heat, set aside and keep warm.

- Meanwhile, combine all spice paste ingredients in a small bowl. Mix until pasty, adding extra lemon juice, if necessary. Set aside.

- Melt ghee in a large frying pan (skillet) over moderate heat. When foam subsides, add potatoes and aubergine. Fry for 5 minutes, stirring frequently.

- Add spice paste and fry for 10 minutes, stirring constantly. Add 1–2 Tbsp water, if mixture is too dry.

- Cover pan, reduce heat to low and cook vegetables for 15–20 minutes or until tender; test by piercing with tip of a sharp knife. When done, remove pan from heat and set aside.

- Spread half the rice over base of an ovenproof (flameproof) dish. Sprinkle half the melted butter over.

- Spread vegetable mixture over rice and cover with remaining rice. Sprinkle remaining melted butter over.

- Cover dish and bake in a preheated oven at 180°C (350°F) for 20–25 minutes or until ingredients are very hot.

- Remove from oven and serve immediately from dish.

To degorge aubergines, sprinkle salt onto cut surfaces and stand for 30 minutes before rinsing thoroughly. This will reduce the amount of oil absorbed during cooking.

pilaf with pineapple and cashew nuts

A subtle blend of tastes and textures makes this pilaf an exciting accompaniment to roast lamb. Alternatively, serve it on its own, accompanied by a green salad.

Serves 4

Ingredients

Butter	90 g (3 oz)
Pineapple	1, small, peeled, cored and cut into chunks
Raisins	3 Tbsp
Spring onions (scallions)	12, chopped
Cashew nuts	75 g (2½ oz)
Coriander seeds	1 Tbsp, coarsely crushed
Cayenne pepper	¼ tsp
Long-grain rice	360 g (12 oz), washed, soaked in cold water for 30 minutes and drained
Salt	1 tsp or more to taste
Vegetable or chicken stock	625 ml (1 pint / 2½ cups)

Garnishing

Eggs	2, hard-boiled, shelled and quartered
Chopped coriander leaves (cilantro)	1 Tbsp

Method

- Melt half the butter in a medium frying pan (skillet) over moderate heat. When foam subsides, add pineapple and raisins. Fry for 2–3 minutes, turning frequently.

- When pineapple is lightly coloured, remove pan from heat and set aside.

- Melt remaining butter in a large saucepan over moderate heat. When foam subsides, add spring onions. Fry, stirring occasionally, for 4–5 minutes or until golden brown.

- Add cashew nuts, coriander seeds and cayenne pepper. Fry for about 4 minutes, stirring occasionally.

- Add rice and salt. Fry mixture, stirring constantly, for 5 minutes. Stir in pineapple and raisins, then add stock and bring to the boil.

- Cover pan, reduce heat to low and cook for 20–25 minutes or until rice is tender and all the liquid has been absorbed.

- Adjust seasoning to taste, then remove pan from heat. Spoon pilaf onto a serving platter.

- Garnish as desired and serve immediately.

italian braised rice with mushrooms

This is an attractive risotto dish of rice, mushrooms, onion and grated cheese. Use a mixture of mushroom types and include a few porcini (cep) mushrooms for a meaty taste and a hearty meal.

Serves 4–6

Ingredients

Butter	90 g (3 oz) butter
Onion	1, medium, peeled and finely chopped
Garlic	1 clove, peeled and crushed
Italian rice	450 g (1 lb), use Arborio or similar
Dry white wine	90 ml (3 fl oz)
Vegetable or beef stock	1.25 litres (2 pints / 5 cups), boiling hot
Mushrooms of choice	300 g (10 oz), wiped clean and sliced
Freshly grated nutmeg	½–1 tsp
Cayenne pepper	½ tsp
Salt	½ tsp or to taste
Freshly ground black pepper	¼ tsp or to taste
Parmesan cheese	60 g (2 oz), grated

Method

• Melt 60 g (2 oz) butter in a large, heavy saucepan over moderate heat. When foam subsides, add onion and garlic. Cook, stirring occasionally, for 5–7 minutes or until onion is soft and translucent but not brown.

• Add rice to pan, reduce heat to low and cook for 5 minutes, stirring frequently.

• Add wine and about one-third of stock. Regulate heat so that mixture is constantly bubbling. Stir occasionally with a fork.

• When rice swells and all the liquid has been absorbed, add another third of stock and regulate heat again. Repeat with last third of stock and rice should be tender and moist but still firm at the end.

• Stir in mushrooms, nutmeg, cayenne pepper and seasoning. Adjust to taste and cook for about 3 minutes, stirring occasionally.

• Add remaining butter and cheese. Stir to mix well and simmer for 1 minute, stirring frequently.

• Remove pan from heat, dish out and serve immediately. Sprinkle extra cayenne pepper over, if desired.

italian braised rice with courgettes

Serve this appetising and delicious risotto with some garlic bread for a satisfying vegetarian meal. If preferred, use chicken stock for a richer flavour.

Serves 4–6

Ingredients

Butter	120 g (4 oz)
Garlic	2 cloves, peeled and crushed
Courgettes (zucchini)	450 g (1 lb), small, trimmed, washed and thinly sliced
Salt	1 tsp or to taste
Freshly ground black pepper	1 tsp or to taste
Canned peeled tomatoes	420 g (14 oz)
Dry white wine	150 ml (5 fl oz)
Italian rice	450 g (1 lb) use Arborio or similar
Vegetable or chicken stock	940 ml (1½ pints / 3¾ cups), boiling hot
Parmesan cheese	60 g (2 oz / ½ cup), grated

Method

- Melt 90 g (3 oz) butter in a large, heavy saucepan over moderate heat. When foam subsides, add garlic and cook, stirring constantly, for 1 minute.

- Add courgettes and cook, stirring and turning occasionally, for 10–12 minutes or until lightly and evenly browned.

- Stir in seasoning to taste, tomatoes with can juices and wine. Bring to the boil, stirring constantly.

- Add rice, reduce heat to low and cook, stirring frequently, for 5 minutes.

- Add about one-third of stock. Regulate heat so that mixture is constantly bubbling. Stir occasionally with a fork.

- When rice swells and all the liquid has been absorbed, add another third of stock and regulate heat again. Repeat with last third of stock and rice should be tender and moist but still firm at the end.

- Stir in remaining butter and cheese. Mix well and simmer for 1 minute, stirring frequently.

- Remove from heat and serve immediately.

spanish rice with mushrooms and capsicums

This may be served hot or cold as a side dish to grilled (broiled) meat or fish. Alternatively, it may be served with crusty bread and a mixed salad for a light lunch.

Serves 3–4

Ingredients

Olive oil	3 Tbsp
Onions	2, peeled and thinly sliced
Garlic	1 clove, peeled and crushed
Green capsicum (bell pepper)	1, seeded, pith removed and thinly sliced
Red capsicums	2, seeded, pith removed and thinly sliced
Mushrooms of choice	360 g (12 oz), wiped clean and sliced
Canned peeled tomatoes	420 g (14 oz), chopped
Pitted green olives	45 g (1½ oz / ½ cup)
Dried oregano	1 tsp
Dried basil	½ tsp
Salt	½ tsp or to taste
Freshly ground black pepper	¼ tsp or to taste
Cooked rice	480 g (16 oz / 2 cups)

Method

- Heat oil in a large frying pan (skillet) over moderate heat. Cook onions and garlic, stirring occasionally, for 5–7 minutes or until onions are soft and translucent but not brown.

- Add capsicums and cook for 4 minutes, stirring frequently.

- Add mushrooms, tomatoes with can juices, olives, oregano, basil and seasoning to taste. Cook for 3 minutes, stirring occasionally.

- Add rice and cook, stirring constantly, for 3–4 minutes or until rice is heated through.

- Dish out and serve immediately, if serving hot. Set aside to cool, if serving cold.

indian tomato rice

Simple, tasty and nutritious, this dish is an excellent accompaniment to curries, roast chicken or lamb.

Serves 6

Ingredients

Butter	3 Tbsp
Onions	2, medium, peeled and finely chopped
Garlic	1 clove, peeled and crushed
Ginger	2.5-cm (1-in) knob, peeled and finely chopped
Red capsicum (bell pepper)	1, seeded, pith removed and finely sliced
Long-grain rice	360 g (12 oz / 2 cups), washed, soaked in water for 30 minutes and drained
Canned peeled tomatoes	420 g (14 oz), finely chopped
Salt	1 tsp or to taste
Freshly ground black pepper	¼ tsp or to taste
Spring onions (scallions)	2, thinly sliced

Method

- Melt butter in a large saucepan over moderate heat. When foam subsides, add onions, garlic and ginger. Fry, stirring occasionally, for 5–7 minutes or until onions are soft and translucent but not brown.

- Add capsicum and fry for 3 minutes, stirring occasionally.

- Add rice and fry for 3 minutes, stirring constantly.

- Add tomatoes and can juices, then top with water until liquid covers rice by 1-cm (½-in). Season to taste and bring to the boil.

- When liquid is boiling vigorously, cover pan and reduce heat to very low. Simmer for 15–20 minutes or until rice is tender and all the liquid has been absorbed.

- Remove from heat and dish out, then garnish with spring onions and serve immediately.

seafood

nasi ulam
(malay herb rice)

This is an abbreviated version of the traditional dish, which is intensely laborious to prepare and requires many herbs—such as polygonum (laksa), turmeric (kunyit) and lesser galangal (kencur) leaves—that are no longer readily available.

Serves 2

Ingredients

Cooking oil	2 Tbsp
Salted fish	50 g (2 oz), thinly sliced
Sambal belacan	1 Tbsp or more to taste
Shallots	2, peeled and thinly sliced
Lime juice	60 ml (2 fl oz / 4 Tbsp)
Cooked long-grain rice	400 g (13½ oz)
Salt	1 tsp or to taste
White cabbage	100 g (3½ oz), thinly sliced, blanched and drained
Cucumbers	150 g (5 oz), peeled, cored and shredded
Coriander leaves (cilantro)	5 sprigs, chopped
Fresh basil leaves	100 g (3½ oz), shredded
Kaffir lime leaves (*daun limau purut*)	4 or more to taste, shredded
Crisp-fried shallots	

Method

- Heat oil in a wok and fry salted fish until crisp and fragrant. Drain and leave to cool completely, then pound until fine and set aside.

- Prepare dressing. Combine *sambal belacan*, shallots and lime juice in a small bowl. Mix well.

- Put rice into a large mixing bowl and add all remaining ingredients, except crisp-fried shallots.

- Toss ingredients together with dressing until evenly mixed.

- Serve garnished with crisp-fried shallots.

Sambal belacan is a pasty condiment often seen on Malay and Peranakan (Straits Chinese) tables. *Sambal* refers to a condiment made essentially of red chillies and *belacan* – a pungent, dried prawn (shrimp) paste. Ready-made *sambal belacan* is available at most supermarkets or Asian stores.

japanese rice in green tea with salmon

Easy to prepare and elegant, this dish makes a great starter and is bound to be a topic of conversation.

Serves 4

Ingredients

Salmon fillet	180 g (6 oz), skinned and sliced
Salt	1 tsp
Cooked Japanese rice	250 g (9 oz), kept warm
Hot water	800 ml (26 fl oz / 3¼ cups)
Green tea leaves	1 Tbsp
Japanese light soy sauce	1 Tbsp or to taste
Japanese seaweed (nori) strips	to taste

Method

- Pan-fry salmon until lightly browned and cooked, seasoning to taste with salt. Remove and set aside.
- Divide rice equally among individual bowls and top each with a few salmon slices.
- Prepare green tea. Pour hot water over tea leaves and allow to infuse for about 1 minute, then strain and pour over rice.
- Drizzle with soy sauce and sprinkle seaweed strips over. Serve immediately.

futomaki
(thick-rolled sushi)

For a more authentic but also more tangy and pungent flavour, replace cucumber in this recipe with takuan—*Japanese pickled radish (daikon), usually bright yellow.*

Makes 2 rolls

Ingredients

Prawns (shrimps)	6, medium, shelled and deveined
Japanese seaweed (nori)	2 sheets
Cucumber	1, peeled, cored and cut into 1-cm (½-in) wide strips
Mayonnaise	1½ Tbsp
Wasabi	to taste
Japanese light soy sauce	to taste

Omelette

Eggs	2, beaten
Dashi	1½ Tbsp
Salt	a pinch
Cooking oil	

Sushi Rice (Vinegared Rice)

Japanese rice	200 g (7 oz)
Water	250 ml (8 fl oz / 1 cup)
Japanese rice vinegar	2 Tbsp
Sugar	1 Tbsp
Salt	2 tsp

Method

- Prepare sushi rice. Wash rice thoroughly, until water runs clear. Drain and set aside for 1 hour.
- Combine rice and water in a rice cooker and set to cook. When rice is done, switch off cooker and leave covered.
- Combine vinegar, sugar and salt in a small bowl. Stir until sugar and salt are dissolved.
- Drizzle mixture evenly into rice and lightly fold rice to mix well. Leave rice to cool before using.
- Meanwhile, prepare omelette. Combine eggs, stock and salt in a bowl, beating to mix well.
- Heat oil in a non-stick pan and pour in just enough egg to cover base. When omelette sets, fold in half and leave in pan.
- Grease empty half of pan and pour in more egg mixture. Lift first omelette to allow egg mixture to run underneath, then replace.
- When second omelette is lightly set, fold it over the first. Repeat process until egg mixture is used up.
- Remove finished omelette and cool completely before cutting into 1-cm (½-in) wide strips.
- Bring a small, deep pot of salted water to the boil. Meanwhile, push a skewer through the length of each prawn; this is so that they remain straight after cooking.

- Dip skewered prawns into boiling water and remove when pink. Drain and leave to cool. Remove skewers before using.

- To assemble sushi, place a sheet of seaweed on a sushi-rolling mat. Spread half the cooled rice onto it, leaving a 2-cm (1-in) margin along top and bottom edges.

- Make a shallow, trough depression across the centre of rice. Moisten fingers to prevent rice from sticking.

- Spread half the mayonnaise along the trough, then top with a few cucumber strips, omelette and prawns.

- Use mat to lift and roll seaweed and rice over filling firmly. Unwrap mat and make another roll.

- Slice each roll into 8 rounds using a sharp knife. Wipe knife with a damp tea towel after each cut to ensure clean, neat slices.

- Serve with wasabi and soy sauce on the side.

chinese seafood fried rice

A combination of seafood and common store-cupboard items makes this a great-tasting and quick-to-prepare dish. Seafood takes very little time to cook.

Serves 4

Ingredients

Long-grain rice	240 g (8 oz), washed, soaked in cold water for 30 minutes and drained
Water	500 ml (16 fl oz / 2 cups)
Salt	1½ tsp
Cooking oil	2 Tbsp
Onions	2, medium, peeled and finely chopped
Cooked ham	120 g (4 oz), finely chopped
Baby peas	2 Tbsp
Tomatoes	2, medium, blanched, peeled and quartered
Prawns (shrimps)	240 g (8 oz), parboiled and shelled
Squid tubes	180 g (6 oz), cut into rings and parboiled
Light soy sauce	1 Tbsp or to taste
Ground white pepper	to taste
Egg	1, lightly beaten

Method

- Put rice in a medium, heavy saucepan. Add water and add 1 tsp salt. Bring to the boil over high heat.

- Reduce heat to low, cover and simmer for 15 minutes or until all the water has been absorbed. Remove from heat. Alternatively, use a rice cooker.

- Heat oil in a large saucepan over moderate heat. Fry onions for 2 minutes, stirring constantly.

- Add ham, peas, tomatoes, prawns, squid and remaining salt. Cook for 1 minute, stirring constantly.

- Stir in cooked rice and cook for 2 minutes, still stirring constantly. Add soy sauce and pepper, adjusting to taste.

- Make a well in the ingredients and add egg. Briskly fold ingredients in towards liquid egg and stir continuously for 2 minutes.

- Remove from heat and serve immediately.

nasi lemak
(malay coconut rice)

A traditional Malay dish, nasi lemak *is a breakfast favourite in Southeast Asia and typically includes fried fish, an omelette and sweet* sambal, *a chilli-based condiment. Ready-made sweet* sambal *can be bought at most supermarkets and Asian stores.*

Serves 4

Ingredients

Long-grain rice	450 g (1 lb)
Coconut milk	750 ml (24 fl oz / 3 cups)
Salt	a pinch
Screwpine (*pandan*) leaves	2–3, washed and knotted
Cucumber	½, peeled and sliced into thin rounds

Sweet Sambal

Dried chillies	50 g (1½ oz), softened in water and cut into short lengths
Shallots	50 g (1½ oz), peeled and roughly chopped
Dried prawn (shrimp) paste (*belacan*)	1 tsp
Cooking oil	120 ml (4 fl oz / ½ cup)
Sugar	2 Tbsp
Tamarind pulp (*asam Jawa*)	1 Tbsp, mixed with 4 Tbsp water and strained
Salt	to taste

Fried Fish

Yellow-banded scads (*ikan kuning*)	500 g (1 lb 1½ oz), cleaned
Salt	1 tsp
Ground turmeric	1½ tsp
Cooking oil for deep-frying	

Omelette

Cooking oil	
Eggs	3, beaten
Salt	a pinch
Light soy sauce	1 tsp

Method

- Combine rice and coconut milk in a rice cooker. Sprinkle in salt and place screwpine leaves on top. Set to cook and when done, discard screwpine leaves. Leave rice in pot to keep warm.

- Prepare sweet *sambal*. Combine dried chilles, shallots and prawn paste in a blender (processor) until fine.

- Heat oil in a wok and fry paste until fragrant. Add sugar, tamarind juice and salt to taste. Cook until *sambal* thickens, then remove and set aside to cool.

- Season fish with salt and turmeric. Leave for 10–15 minutes. Heat oil for deep-frying and lower fish in to cook. When done, remove to absorbent paper to drain.

- Prepare omelette. Combine eggs, salt and soy sauce in a bowl and beat well. Heat oil in a shallow frying pan (skillet), then pour in eggs to make a thin omelette. Remove from heat and cut into desired serving-size pieces.

- Scoop rice onto individual serving plates and add desired amounts of sweet *sambal*, deep-fried fish, omelette and cucumber slices.

italian rice with prawns and mushrooms

Italian rice, unlike basmati or patna, needs no washing or soaking. The amount of cooking liquid required depends on the type of rice used. Arborio and basmati, for example, are able to absorb more water without turning mushy.

Serves 4

Ingredients

Butter	60 g (2 oz)
Olive oil	2 Tbsp
Onion	1, large, peeled and finely chopped
Garlic	1 clove, peeled and finely chopped
Red capsicum (bell pepper)	1, medium, seeded, pith removed and sliced
Button mushrooms	120 g (4 oz), wiped clean and chopped
Dried basil	½ tsp
Salt	1 tsp or to taste
Freshly ground black pepper	½ tsp or to taste
Italian rice	360 g (12 oz), use Arborio or similar
Shelled prawns (shrimps)	360 g (12 oz), deveined
Fish stock or water	940 ml (1½ pints / 3¾ cups), boiling hot
Parmesan cheese	60 g (2 oz / ½ cup), grated

Method

- Melt half the butter with oil in a large frying pan (skillet) over moderately high heat. When foam subsides, reduce heat to moderate.

- Add onion, garlic and capsicum. Fry, stirring occasionally, for 5–7 minutes or until onion is soft and translucent but not brown.

- Stir in mushrooms, basil and seasoning to taste. Cook for 5 minutes, stirring occasionally.

- Add rice, reduce heat to low and cook, stirring frequently, for 5 minutes, then stir in prawns and cook for 1 minute.

- Add about one-third of stock or water. Regulate heat so that mixture is constantly bubbling. Stir occasionally with a fork.

- When rice swells and all the liquid is absorbed, add another third of stock or water and regulate heat again.

- Repeat with last third of stock; rice should be tender and moist at the end. If not, add more liquid and continue cooking.

- When rice is cooked, remove from heat. Stir in remaining butter and cheese, then serve immediately.

paella
(spanish rice with seafood and chicken)

Traditional paella is made with a combination of chicken, seafood, sausage, vegetables and rice. It can vary from a simple supper dish of chicken and a handful of prawns to an elaborate party dish with lobster and mussels.

Serves 4–6

Ingredients

Cooked lobster	1, about 675 g (1½ lb), tail shell split, claws cracked and grey sac removed
Olive oil	2 Tbsp
Chicken	1, about 900 g (2 lb), cut into 8 pieces
Chorizo (spicy pork sausage)	1, sliced
Onion	1, medium, peeled and thinly sliced
Garlic	1 clove, peeled and crushed
Tomatoes	3, blanched, peeled, seeded and chopped, or 240 g (8 oz) canned peeled tomatoes, drained
Red capsicum (bell pepper)	1, large, seeded, pith removed and chopped
Salt	1 tsp or to taste
Freshly ground black pepper	½ tsp or to taste
Paprika	1 tsp or to taste
Long-grain rice	360 g (12 oz), washed, soaked in water for 30 minutes and drained
Water	625 ml (1 pint / 2½ cups)
Lemon juice	squeezed from 1 lemon
Saffron threads	1 tsp, soaked in 125 ml (4 fl oz / ½ cup) warm water for 20 minutes
Peas	240 g (8 oz)
Prawns (shrimps)	180 g (6 oz), large, shelled and deveined
Mussels	500 g (1 lb 1½ oz), scrubbed clean and steamed until cooked
Chopped parsley	1 Tbsp

Method

- Remove lobster meat from tail shell and claws. Cut into 2.5-cm (1-in) pieces and set aside.

- Heat olive oil in a large pan or heatproof (flameproof) casserole over moderate heat. Fry chicken and chorizo, turning occasionally, for 10–15 minutes or until chicken is evenly browned.

- Use tongs or a slotted spoon to remove solid ingredients from pan. Set side and keep warm.

- Add onion and garlic to pan and fry, stirring occasionally, for 5–7 minutes or until onion is soft and translucent but not brown.

- Add tomatoes, capsicum and seasoning to taste. Cook, stirring occasionally, for 10–12 minutes or until mixture is thick.

- Add rice and fry, shaking pan frequently, for 3 minutes or until rice turns transparent.

- Add water, lemon juice and saffron mixture. Bring to the boil, then reduce heat to low and stir in peas.

- Return chicken and sausage to pan and cook for 15 minutes, stirring occasionally.

- Add lobster meat, prawns and mussels. Cook for a further 5 minutes or until chicken is cooked through and most of the cooking liquid has been absorbed.

- Remove from heat and let stand for about 5 minutes; the dish will dry out as it cools. Sprinkle parsley over before serving.

italian saffron rice with seafood

Quick to prepare because seafood cooks in minutes, this dish is flavoured by the classic combination of garlic, white wine and stock.

Serves 4–6

Ingredients

Butter	120 g (4 oz)
Onion	1, medium, peeled and thinly sliced
Garlic	1 clove, peeled and crushed
Italian rice	450 g (1 lb), use Arborio or similar
Dry white wine	90 ml (3 fl oz)
Chicken stock	1.25 litres (2 pints / 5 cups), boiling hot
Prawns (shrimps)	250 g (9 oz), shelled and deveined
Scallops	250 g (9 oz), rinsed, drained and halved
Saffron threads	1 tsp, crushed and soaked in 1½ Tbsp hot water
Parmesan cheese	60 g (2 oz), grated

Method

- Melt 90 g (3 oz) butter in a large, heavy saucepan over moderate heat. When foam subsides, add onion and garlic. Cook, stirring occasionally, for 5–7 minutes or until onion is soft and translucent but not brown.

- Add rice, reduce heat to low and cook for 5 minutes, stirring frequently.

- Add wine and about one-third of stock. Regulate heat so that mixture is constantly bubbling. Stir occasionally with a fork.

- When rice swells and all the liquid is absorbed, add another third of stock and regulate heat again. Repeat with remaining stock; rice should be tender and moist but still firm at the end.

- Stir in prawns and scallops and cook, stirring, for 2 minutes.

- Stir in saffron mixture, remaining butter and cheese. Mix well and simmer for 1 minute, stirring frequently.

- Remove from heat and serve immediately.

braised rice with shellfish

This dish is not a classic risotto in the Italian style but it is nevertheless a sustaining and memorable meal. Rich with seafood and sweet juices, it is a delight for the whole family.

Serves 4

Ingredients

Mussels	1 kg (2 lb 3 oz), scrubbed clean
Water	600 ml (20 fl oz)
Butter	4 Tbsp
Long-grain rice	240 g (8 oz), washed, soaked in cold water for 30 minutes and drained
Fish stock	250 ml (8 fl oz / 1 cup)
Salt	1½ tsp or to taste
Freshly ground black pepper	1 tsp or to taste
Tomatoes	3, large, blanched, peeled, seeded and chopped
Garlic	2 cloves, peeled and crushed
Plain (all-purpose) flour	1 Tbsp
Dry white wine	250 ml (8 fl oz / 1 cup)
Lemon juice	1 Tbsp
Sweet vermouth	1 Tbsp
Scallops	240 g (8 oz), rinsed and drained
Shelled prawns	240 g (8 oz), large, or langoustines
Parmesan cheese	120 g (4 oz), grated

Method

- Put mussels into a large saucepan and add half the water. Place over high heat and cook, shaking saucepan frequently, until mussels open up.

- When done, remove open mussels with a slotted spoon; discard those unopened. Reserve 125 ml (4 fl oz / ½ cup) of cooking liquid.

- Melt half the butter in a large saucepan over moderate heat. When foam subsides, add rice and fry for 3 minutes, stirring constantly.

- Add fish stock, remaining water, half the salt and pepper, tomatoes and garlic. Bring to the boil, stirring constantly.

- Reduce heat to low, cover pan and simmer for 20 minutes or until rice is tender and has absorbed all the liquid.

- Meanwhile, melt remaining butter in a medium saucepan over moderate heat. Remove from heat, then stir in flour and remaining salt and pepper with a wooden spoon to make a smooth paste.

- Gradually add reserved mussel liquid, wine, lemon juice and vermouth, stirring constantly to avoid lumps.

- Return pan to heat and cook sauce, stirring constantly, for 3 minutes or until smooth and slightly thickened.

- Remove from heat and spoon half the sauce into a warm sauceboat. Set aside and keep warm.

- Return pan to heat again and add mussels, scallops and prawns (shrimps). Cook for 5 minutes, stirring frequently, and adjust seasoning to taste. Remove from heat and keep warm.

- Remove rice from heat and stir in half the cheese, then mix in seafood and sauce. Serve rice mixture in individual serving bowls with remaining cheese in a bowl on the side.

- Alternatively, keep cooked rice and seafood separate— divide rice among individual serving bowls, then ladle seafood with sauce over.

festive pilau

This is a colourful dish of rice, vegetables and prawns. Serve as an accompaniment to Indonesian or East Indian dishes.

Serves 6–8

Ingredients

Butter	4 Tbsp
Onions	2, medium, peeled and finely chopped
Long-grain rice	450 g (1 lb), washed, soaked in cold water for 30 minutes and drained
Salt	1 tsp or to taste
Freshly ground black pepper	½ tsp or to taste
Water	1.5 litres (6 cups)
Desiccated coconut	120 g (4 oz), or 100 g (5 oz) freshly grated coconut
Yellow food colouring	1 tsp
Sweet corn	240 g (8 oz), cooked, drained and kept warm
Green capsicum (bell pepper)	1, large, seeded, pith removed and finely chopped
Green food colouring	¼ tsp
Prawns (shrimps)	240 g (8 oz), shelled, cooked and kept warm
Red food colouring	1 tsp
Eggs	3, hard-boiled, shelled and thinly sliced

Method

- Melt butter in a large saucepan over moderate heat. When foam subsides, add onions and fry, stirring constantly, for 5–7 minutes or until onions are soft and translucent but not brown.

- Stir in rice and cook for a further 2 minutes, then season to taste. Add water, increase heat to high and bring to the boil.

- Reduce heat to low, cover pan and simmer for 15–20 minutes or until rice is tender and all the liquid has been absorbed.

- Remove from heat and divide rice equally among 4 medium mixing bowls. Stir coconut into one bowl.

- Add yellow food colouring and sweet corn to the second bowl and mix well with a fork.

- Add capsicum and green food colouring to the third bowl, and prawns and red food colouring to the last. Mix well each time.

- Serve each colour separately and as desired, garnishing with egg slices.

- For a more conservative serving suggestion, arrange coloured rice on a large serving platter, in four different sections, with egg slices separating each section.

squid stuffed with rice

A tasty and unusual dish, Squid Stuffed with Rice is an adaptation of a famous Greek recipe. Serve hot or cold with a crisp, green salad and some chilled white wine.

Serves 6

Ingredients

Squids	6, large
Salt	2 tsp
Freshly ground black pepper	½ tsp
Garlic	1 clove, peeled and crushed
Tomato juice	125 ml (4 fl oz / ½ cup)
Olive oil	125 ml (4 fl oz / ½ cup)
Onions	2, medium, peeled and finely chopped
Long-grain rice	60 g (2 oz), washed, soaked in cold water for 30 minutes and drained
Chopped parsley	2 Tbsp
Chopped mint	2 Tbsp
Chopped walnuts	1 Tbsp
White wine	180 ml (6 fl oz / ¾ cup)
Chicken stock	180 ml (6 fl oz / ¾ cup)
Plain (all-purpose) flour	1½ Tbsp
Butter	2 Tbsp

Method

- Clean squids. Pull off heads, then reserve and finely chop tentacles. Discard remainder.

- Remove and discard quills, wings and purple skins. Wash and drain squid tubes, then sprinkle half the salt and pepper inside. Set aside.

- Combine garlic, tomato juice and half the olive oil in a large mixing bowl. Beat mixture with a fork, then add squid tubes and stir until well coated. Leave to marinate for 1 hour.

- Heat remaining oil in a frying pan (skillet) over moderate heat. Add onions and cook, stirring occasionally, for 5–7 minutes or until soft and translucent but not brown.

- Stir in tentacles, remaining salt and pepper, rice, parsley, mint and walnuts. Cook mixture for 5 minutes, stirring frequently. Remove from heat and set aside.

- Remove squid from tomato mixture with a slotted spoon. Reserve tomato mixture.

- Half-fill each squid tube with rice mixture. Secure opening of each squid with two cocktail sticks.

- Place squid in a heatproof (flameproof) casserole. Add tomato mixture, wine and stock.

- Bake in a preheated oven at 180°C (350°F), on the centre shelf, for 40–50 minutes or until squid is tender. Test by piercing with tip of a sharp knife.

- When done, remove casserole from oven, transfer squid to a cutting board and slice as desired. Arrange squid pieces on a serving plate and set aside.

- Place casserole over moderate heat. Rub flour into butter until well combined, then add to casserole, a little at a time, stirring constantly.

- Cook sauce for 3 minutes or until slightly thickened, then remove casserole from heat.

- Spoon sauce over squid and serve immediately, if serving hot.

chinese fish soup with rice

The delicate taste of fresh fish is enhanced with the fragrance of ginger and the tang of tomatoes. While freshwater fish can be used, seawater varieties are tastier.

Serves 2–3

Ingredients

Fish fillet	500 g (1 lb 1½ oz), thinly sliced, use snapper, grouper or similar
Light soy sauce	2 tsp or to taste
Cooking oil	1 Tbsp
Garlic	1 clove, peeled and crushed
Water	750 ml (24 fl oz/3 cups)
Ginger	1-cm (½-in) knob, peeled and shredded
Corn flour (cornstarch)	2 tsp, mixed with 4 Tbsp water
Egg	1, lightly beaten
Tomatoes	2, cut into wedges
Coriander leaves (cilantro)	1 sprig, chopped
Cooked long-grain rice	500 g (1 lb 1½ oz)
Red chillies	3, seeded and thinly sliced
Red chilli strips (optional) for garnishing	

Method

- Season fish slices with soy sauce to taste. Leave for 10 minutes.
- Heat oil in a pot and stir-fry garlic until fragrant.
- Add water and bring to the boil, then add ginger and fish slices.
- Stir in corn flour solution to thicken soup lightly.
- Lower heat until soup is just simmering. Pour in egg while stirring so that egg ribbons are formed.
- Add tomatoes and coriander. Turn off heat when tomatoes are tender, but not mushy.
- Spoon rice onto deep plates, ladle soup and ingredients over.
- Serve hot with a side dip of chillies in soy sauce, and garnished with chilli strips, if using.

poultry

chinese steamed glutinous rice

This classic Chinese dish is intensely flavourful and aromatic. It can make either a hearty snack or a light meal.

Ingredients

Chicken meat	500 g (1 lb 1½ oz), cut into slices
Cooking oil	2 Tbsp
Dried Chinese mushrooms	80 g (3 oz), soaked to soften, stems discarded and cut into strips
Glutinous rice	1 kg (2 lb 3 oz), washed and drained
Salt	1½ tsp
Dark soy sauce	1 tsp
Light soy sauce	1 tsp
Five-spice powder	1 tsp
Ground white pepper	1 tsp
Water	1 litre (32 fl oz / 4 cups)
Coriander leaves (cilantro)	1 sprig
Chilli sauce of choice	

Seasoning

Oyster sauce	3 Tbsp
Dark soy sauce	2 tsp
Light soy sauce	2 tsp
Ground white pepper	2 tsp

Method

- Combine seasoning ingredients and mix in chicken. Leave for 1 hour, refrigerated.

- Heat cooking oil in a wok or large pan. Stir-fry mushrooms for 2–3 minutes. Drain and set aside.

- Reheat wok or pan and add rice. Stir-fry and season with salt, both soy sauces, five-spice powder and pepper. Add water and simmer for 10 minutes until rice is partially cooked. Remove from heat.

- Grease some heatproof (flameproof) bowls. Line each one with chicken and mushrooms, then fill three-quarters way with glutinous rice, packing in tightly.

- Steam bowls over rapidly boiling water for 45 minutes or until rice is well done. Turn out onto serving plates to serve. Alternatively, scoop out from steaming bowls.

- Garnish with coriander and serve with chilli sauce.

chicken congee

A comfort food to many Chinese, chicken congee is easy to put together and easily digestible. Leftover boiled or roasted chicken may be used.

Ingredients

Chicken breasts	2
Salt	1 tsp
Ground white pepper	1 tsp
Water	1.5 litres (48 fl oz / 6 cups)
Long-grain rice	200 g (7 oz), washed and drained

Garnishing

Crisp-fried shallots
Shredded ginger
Chopped spring onions (scallions)
Sliced red chillies
Ground white pepper
Light soy sauce
Sesame oil

Method

- Season chicken with salt and pepper and set aside for 20 minutes, refrigerated.

- Combine seasoned chicken and water in a pot. Bring to the boil and simmer for 15 minutes or until chicken is cooked. Remove from heat.

- If time permits, leave chicken to cool in stock. Otherwise, drain and set aside to cool, reserving stock.

- Add rice to stock and bring to the boil. Reduce heat and simmer, partially covered, for 45–60 minutes or until rice is soft and broken up. Stir occasionally to prevent sticking.

- Meanwhile, remove and discard chicken skin, if still attached. Shred chicken meat and discard bones, if any.

- Ladle congee into individual serving bowls. Top with chicken and desired amounts of each garnishing ingredient. Alternatively, serve garnishing ingredients on the side for diners to adjust to their own taste.

rice croquettes

Extremely flavourful, these fried rice balls require considerable preparation. For an easier version, see Suppli *(Italian Stuffed Rice Balls) on page 92.*

Serves 4

Ingredients

Cooked Italian rice	240 g (8 oz / 3 cups), use Aborio or similar
Salt	½ tsp or to taste
Freshly ground black pepper	½ tsp or to taste
Butter	4 Tbsp, melted + 1 Tbsp
Parmesan cheese	60 g (2 oz), grated
Eggs	2, well beaten
Shallot	1, peeled and finely chopped
Prosciutto	60 g (2 oz), finely chopped
Chicken livers	60 g (2 oz), cleaned and finely chopped
Dried oregano	¼ tsp
Tomato purée	1 tsp
Mozzarella cheese	60 g (2 oz), finely diced
Breadcrumbs	90 g (3 oz)
Cooking oil for deep-frying	

Method

- Combine rice, seasoning, melted butter, Parmesan cheese and half the eggs in a mixing bowl. Mix well and set aside.

- Heat remaining butter in a frying pan (skillet) over moderate heat. When foam subsides, add shallot, prosciutto, livers and oregano. Cook, stirring frequently, for 4–6 minutes or until shallot is soft and translucent but not brown.

- Stir in tomato purée and continue cooking, stirring constantly, until purée has been absorbed.

- Transfer pan mixture to a small bowl using a slotted spoon. Set aside and leave to cool completely.

- Set a large piece of cling film (plastic wrap) on a clean work surface. Place 1 rounded (heaped) Tbsp rice mixture onto the centre. Spread it out into a circle about 7.5-cm (3-in) in diameter.

- Top with 1 tsp liver mixture and a few mozzarella cubes, then lift cling film (plastic wrap) and mould rice around filling, shaping into a ball. Repeat until ingredients are used up.

- Transfer remaining egg to a plate and breadcrumbs to another. Dip each croquette in egg, then coat with breadcrumbs. Shake off excess and set aside.

- Heat sufficient oil for deep-frying in a large pan; a small cube of stale bread dropped into pan should turn golden in 55 seconds.

- Alternatively, preheat deep-fryer to 180°C (350°F) and dip basket into hot oil before placing croquettes inside.

- Lower in croquettes, a few at a time, and reduce heat to moderate. Fry for 5–6 minutes or until crisp and golden.

- Remove and drain on absorbent paper. Keep cooked croquettes warm while frying remaining ones.

- Serve as soon as last batch is drained.

cantonese clay pot rice

Known to the Cantonese as sar poh farn, *this is a classic one-pot meal made especially appetising by crisp-fried salted fish and Chinese sausages.*

Ingredients

Chicken meat	400 g (14 oz), cut into cubes
Light soy sauce	1 tsp
Oyster sauce	2 tsp
Ground white pepper	1 tsp
Cooking oil	4 Tbsp
Salted fish	10 g ($1/3$ oz), thinly sliced
Shallots	2, peeled and sliced
Dried Chinese mushrooms	80 g (3 oz), soaked to soften, stems discarded and sliced
Chinese sausages	2, thinly sliced
Rice	300 g (10½ oz), washed and drained
Coriander leaves (cilantro)	1 sprig

Sauce (combined)

Water	750 ml (24 fl oz / 3 cups)
Salt	½ tsp
Dark soy sauce	1 tsp
Light soy sauce	1 tsp
Oyster sauce	2 tsp
Ground white pepper	1 tsp

Method

- Season chicken with soy sauce, oyster sauce and pepper. Set aside for 20 minutes, refrigerated.

- Heat 2 Tbsp cooking oil in a wok and fry salted fish until crisp and fragrant. Drain well and set aside.

- Reheat wok and add remaining oil. Stir-fry shallots until fragrant, then add mushrooms and sausages. Cook for 2 minutes.

- Add chicken and stir-fry for 2 minutes or until lightly cooked. Add combined sauce ingredients and bring to the boil, then remove from heat.

- Grease a clay pot and add rice. Top with stir-fried ingredients, including sauce, and crisp-fried salted fish.

- Place clay pot over medium–low heat and leave to cook for 30–45 minutes or until rice is well done.

- Either serve directly from clay pot or scoop out onto individual serving bowls. Serve garnished with coriander.

teochew yam rice

This is an abbreviated version of the classic Teochew dish. The yam imparts a nutty flavour and provides added texture to the dish.

Ingredients

Chicken meat	400 g (13½ oz), cut into small cubes
Cooking oil	500 ml (16 fl oz / 2 cups)
Yam (taro)	300 g (10½ oz), peeled and cut into small cubes
Dried prawns (shrimps)	80 g (2½ oz), soaked for 15 minutes, drained and chopped
Long-grain rice	300 g (10½ oz), washed and drained
Light soy sauce	2 tsp or to taste
Chicken stock	875 ml (29 fl oz / 3½ cups)

Seasoning (combined)

Salt	½ tsp
Ground white pepper	½ tsp
Light soy sauce	1 tsp

Side dip (combined)

Slice red chillies

Light soy sauce

Garnishing

Chopped spring onions (scallions)

Crisp-fried shallots

Red chilli strips

Method

- Combine seasoning ingredients and mix in chicken. Leave for 10 minutes.
- Heat oil in a wok and stir-fry yam cubes for about 10 minutes or until just cooked. Drain and set aside.
- Remove oil from wok, leaving behind about 2 Tbsp. Reheat and stir-fry dried prawns until fragrant. Drain and set aside.
- Add rice to wok and stir-fry for 5 minutes. Remove and place into a rice cooker with soy sauce, stock, chicken, yam and dried prawns. Stir to mix ingredients, then set to cook.
- Serve garnished as desired and with a side dip of sliced red chillies in light soy sauce.

japanese rice with egg and chicken

Quick and easy to prepare, this one-dish meal is a fuss-free and tasty way to complete a long day at work.

Ingredients

Dashi	250 ml (8 fl oz / 1 cup)
Sugar	1 Tbsp
Mirin	4 Tbsp
Japanese light soy sauce	4 Tbsp
Large onion	1, peeled and thinly sliced into rings
Chicken fillet	250 g (8½ oz), cut into small cubes
Eggs	4, large, lightly beaten
Cooked Japanese rice	300 g (10 oz), kept warm
Nanami togarashi	to taste

Method

- Combine dashi, sugar, mirin and soy sauce in a bowl. Pour into a medium frying pan (skillet) with a lid and bring to the boil.

- Add onion rings and chicken cubes and turn heat up to high. Cook for 2–3 minutes, shaking pan frequently to ensure chicken is evenly cooked.

- Pour in eggs to cover chicken and onion rings. Cover pan and leave for about 30 seconds. Remove from heat and leave to stand for about 1 minute; this allows eggs to cook lightly but remain soft.

- Divide rice evenly among 4 serving bowls. Pour warm egg mixture over each bowl and serve, sprinkled with nanami togarashi, or Japanese seven-spice seasoning, to taste.

yueng chow fried rice

This Chinese dish is named after a province in China and it is so rich with ingredients that it could be a one-dish meal or a luxurious foundation for a Chinese meal.

Serves 4–6

Ingredients

Cooking oil	4 Tbsp
Cooked pork	120 g (4 oz), diced
Cooked chicken	120 g (4 oz), diced
Prawns (shrimps)	120 g (4 oz), shelled and deveined
Dried Chinese mushrooms	4, soaked to soften, stems removed and sliced
Ginger	2.5-cm (1-in) knob, peeled and shredded
Cooked long-grain rice	120 g (4 oz), kept warm
Light soy sauce	4 Tbsp or to taste
Ground white pepper	½ tsp or to taste
Bean sprouts	60 g (2 oz), tailed if desired
Spring onions (scallions)	3, trimmed and chopped
Eggs	2, scrambled and kept warm
Chinese or Iceberg lettuce leaves	6, washed, shaken dry and shredded

Method

- Heat oil in a wok or large pan over moderate heat. Add pork, chicken, prawns, mushrooms and ginger. Stir-fry continuously for 2 minutes.

- Add rice, soy sauce, pepper, bean sprouts and spring onions. Stir-fry until ingredients are well mixed. Adjust seasoning to taste, then remove from heat.

- Stir in eggs, then spoon onto a serving platter or individual serving plates. Garnish with shredded lettuce and serve immediately.

jambalaya
(creole rice with chicken and prawns)

One of most popular Creole dishes from the southern United States, Jambalaya is a delicious dinner party dish. Serve with crusty bread and a tossed green salad.

Serves 4–6

Ingredients

Cooking oil	1 Tbsp
Back bacon	3 slices, chopped
Onion	1, medium, peeled and finely chopped
Celery stalks	2, chopped
Long-grain rice	360 g (12 oz), washed, soaked in cold water for 30 minutes and drained
Chicken stock	625 ml (1 pint / 2½ cups)
Salt	½ tsp or to taste
Freshly ground black pepper	½ tsp or to taste
Cayenne pepper	a dash or to taste
Bay leaf	1, fresh or dried
Shelled prawns (shrimps)	240 g (8 oz)
Chicken meat	240 g (8 oz), cut into small cubes
Green capsicum (bell pepper)	1, large, seeded, pith removed and chopped
Canned peeled tomatoes	420 g (14 oz)
Ham	120 g (4 oz), chopped
Chopped parsley (optional)	1 Tbsp

Method

- Heat oil in a large saucepan over moderate heat. Fry bacon, stirring occasionally, for 5–7 minutes or until crisp and golden brown. Remove with a slotted spoon and drain on absorbent paper.

- Add onion to saucepan and cook, stirring occasionally, for 8–10 minutes or until golden brown.

- Add celery, then rice. Cook, stirring constantly, for 3 minutes or until rice is well coated with bacon fat.

- Gradually add stock, stirring constantly. Add salt, pepper, cayenne pepper and bay leaf. Reduce heat to low, cover pan and simmer for 10 minutes.

- Add prawns, chicken, capsicum and tomatoes, including can juices. Simmer, covered, for 5–7 minutes.

- Add ham and bacon. Stir well, then cover pan again and cook for a further 5–7 minutes or until ingredients are cooked through and rice is tender.

- Remove from heat and serve garnished with parsley, if using.

andalusian chicken

(roast chicken stuffed with ham and rice)

Chicken stuffed with ham and rice, this colourfully-garnished adaptation of a Spanish dish is inexpensive and impressive, but it does take time to prepare.

Serves 4

Ingredients

Chicken	1, large, about 1.8 kg (4 lb)
Butter	4 Tbsp
Olive oil	1 Tbsp
Onion	1, large, peeled
Bouquet garni	1, consisting of 3 sprigs parsley, 1 small bay leaf and 1 sprig thyme tied together, or ½ Tbsp dried bouquet garni
Salt	1 tsp
Freshly ground black pepper	to taste
Plain (all-purpose) flour	1 Tbsp
Tomato purée	2 Tbsp
White wine	125 ml (4 fl oz / ½ cup)

Stuffing

Cooked rice	120 g (4 oz)
Ham	120 g (4 oz), diced
Paprika	2 tsp or to taste
Salt	1 tsp or to taste

Garnishing

Cooking oil	2 Tbsp
Onion	1, large, peeled and sliced in rings
Red capsicum (bell pepper)	1, large, sliced into rings, seeded and pith removed
Green capsicum	1, large, sliced into rings, seeded and pith removed
Tomatoes	450 g (1 lb), peeled and chopped

Method

- Wash chicken inside and out, then pat dry with absorbent paper towels. Set aside.

- Combine all stuffing ingredients in a mixing bowl. Mix well and adjust seasoning to taste, then stuff chicken cavity with mixture. Secure opening with small skewers or cocktail sticks.

- Heat butter and olive oil in a heavy pan. Lightly brown chicken on all sides, then transfer to a roasting pan.

- Add onion, bouquet garni and seasoning to taste. Roast in a preheated oven at 180°C (350°F) for 45–60 minutes.

- Meanwhile, prepare garnishing. Heat oil in a frying pan (skillet) over moderate heat. Sauté onion for 2–3 minutes, then add all remaining ingredients and cook gently until vegetables are soft. Set aside and keep warm.

- When chicken is cooked, remove from oven and transfer to a serving dish. Remove skewers and surround chicken with garnishing ingredients.

- Discard bouquet garni, if using fresh, and onion from roasting pan, then pour pan juices into a saucepan and place over high heat. Sprinkle in flour, stirring constantly with a wooden spoon, then stir in tomato purée and wine.

- Bring to the boil, stirring constantly, then spoon sauce over chicken and serve immediately.

arroz con pollo
(spanish chicken with rice casserole)

A chicken and rice dish from Spain, it is flavoured with garlic and spices. Cooked in a casserole, it makes a delicious main dish.

Serves 4

Ingredients

Cooking oil	3 Tbsp
Streaky bacon	6 slices, chopped
Chicken	1, large, about 2.25 kg (5 lb), or 2 small, cut into serving pieces
Seasoned flour	2 Tbsp
Onions	2, peeled and chopped
Garlic	1 clove, peeled and crushed
Canned tomatoes	420 g (14 oz)
Canned pimientos (all spice)	90 g (3 oz), drained
Paprika	2 tsp
Saffron threads	¼ tsp
Salt	1 tsp or to taste
Water	625 ml (1 pint / 2½ cups)
Long-grain rice	240 g (8 oz)
Frozen peas	180 g (6 oz)
Chopped parsley (optional)	2 Tbsp

Method

- Heat oil in a heatproof (flameproof) casserole over medium heat. Fry bacon for about 5 minutes or until crisp. Remove with a slotted spoon and drain on absorbent paper. Set aside.

- Coat chicken pieces with seasoned flour, shaking off excess and brown in casserole over moderate heat. Remove and set aside.

- Pour out excess oil from casserole and place over moderate heat. Add onions and garlic and fry, stirring occasionally for 2–3 minutes or until onions are soft.

- Place chicken pieces on top and add tomatoes, pimientos, paprika, saffron, salt and water. Increase heat and bring to the boil.

- Add rice and bacon. Stir to mix ingredients, then cover casserole with a piece of aluminium foil and place in a preheated oven at 180°C (350°F) for about 30 minutes.

- Remove casserole from oven, add peas and bake for a further 5–10 minutes or until chicken is tender. If dish is very moist, dry it out by removing the foil cover in the last few minutes of cooking.

- Serve garnished with chopped parsley, if using.

belgian rice with chicken and vegetables

Hearty and nourishing, this dish from Belgium is colourful and appetising, as well as a complete meal in itself.

Serves 4–6

Ingredients

Streaky bacon	6 slices, sliced
Butter	60 g (2 oz)
Chicken breasts	2, skinned, boned and cut into strips
Onions	2, medium, peeled, thinly sliced and pushed out into separate rings
Green capsicums (bell peppers)	2, large, seeded, pith removed and coarsely chopped
Button mushrooms	240 g (8 oz), small, wiped clean and halved
Long-grain rice	300 g (10 oz), washed, soaked in cold water for 30 minutes and drained
Tomatoes	5, medium, blanched, peeled and coarsely chopped
Canned sweet corn	300 g (10 oz), drained
Dried thyme	½ tsp
Salt	1 tsp or to taste
Freshly ground black pepper	½ tsp or to taste
Celery salt	¼ tsp or to taste
Cayenne pepper	¼ tsp or to taste
Worcestershire sauce (optional)	2 tsp
Chicken stock	390 ml (13 fl oz)
Parmesan cheese	60 g (2 oz), grated

Method

- Place a dry, medium heatproof (flameproof) casserole over moderate heat. Fry bacon for 5 minutes or until crisp and golden, and has rendered most of its fat. Scrape bottom of casserole frequently with a spatula to prevent sticking.

- Remove bacon with a slotted spoon and drain on absorbent paper. Set aside on a large plate.

- Add half the butter to casserole. When foam subsides, add chicken strips and fry, stirring frequently, for 6–8 minutes or until lightly browned.

- Remove chicken using a slotted spoon and set aside next to bacon.

- Add onions and capsicums to casserole. Fry for 5 minutes, stirring frequently, then add mushrooms. Fry for a further 3 minutes, still stirring frequently.

- Remove vegetables using slotted spoon and set aside next to chicken.

- Add remaining butter to casserole and when foam subsides, add rice. Fry for 3 minutes, stirring constantly.

- Stir in chicken, bacon and vegetables, tomatoes, sweet corn, thyme, seasoning to taste and Worcestershire sauce, if using. Stir until well mixed.

- Add stock and bring to the boil, stirring constantly. Reduce heat to very low, cover and simmer for 20–25 minutes or until all the liquid has been absorbed and rice is cooked and tender.

- Remove from heat and dish out to a serving platter or divide among individual serving plates. Sprinkle cheese over and serve immediately.

balkan chicken pilaf

This pilaf depends on a strong chicken stock for its flavour. For convenience, cook chicken and make the stock the day before. Serve with a ratatouille and a mixture of yogurt, chopped cucumber and mint leaves for a great contrast and balance of flavours.

Serves 6

Ingredients

Butter	90 g (3 oz)
Onion	1, peeled and finely chopped
Tomatoes	2, peeled and chopped
Salt	1 tsp
Freshly ground black pepper	to taste
Dried basil	1 tsp
Chopped walnuts	60 g (2 oz)
Rice	450 g (1 lb), washed, soaked in water for 30 minutes and drained

Stock

Chicken	1, small
Salt	1 tsp
Onion	1, peeled and halved
Carrots	2, peeled if desired
White peppercorns	4

Garnishing

Chopped cored cucumber

Walnuts

Method

- Prepare stock. Put chicken in a large pot and add enough water to cover it halfway. Add all remaining ingredients and bring to the boil.

- Reduce heat and simmer for 40 minutes or until chicken is tender. Switch off heat and leave chicken to cool in stock.

- Transfer cooled chicken to a clean cutting board and extract all the meat. Put meat into a bowl, cover with cling film (plastic wrap) and refrigerate.

- Return chicken bones to pot and add more water, if necessary, to cover. Simmer for 1½ hours, then strain into a bowl and leave to cool.

- Cover stock with cling film (plastic wrap) and refrigerate until fat surfaces and hardens. Skim off with a spoon.

- Prepare pilaf. Bring 1 litre (32 fl oz / 4 cups) stock to the boil over low heat. Meanwhile, cut chicken meat into strips.

- Melt butter in a large heatproof (flameproof) casserole over moderate heat. Fry onion until golden, then add chicken. Cook, stirring, for 2 minutes.

- Add all remaining ingredients, except rice, and cook for 1 minute. Add rice and cook for 2 minutes, stirring continuously.

- Add hot stock, increase heat and bring to the boil. Cover casserole, reduce heat to very low and simmer for 25 minutes or until all the liquid has been absorbed and rice is cooked. Serve hot.

meat

suppli
(italian stuffed rice balls)

Inspired by Italian cooking, this dish is sometimes known as suppli al telefono *because the melted cheese threads supposedly resemble telephone wires when the balls are pulled apart.*

Makes about 18 balls

Ingredients

Parma ham	120 g (4 oz)
Mozzarella cheese	120 g (4 oz)
Leftover risotto	150 g (5 oz), or plain cooked rice, use Arborio or similar
Eggs	2, lightly beaten
Breadcrumbs	90 g (3 oz)
Cooking oil for deep-frying	

Method

* Cut ham into 2.5-cm (1-in) squares and cheese into 2.5-cm (1-in) cubes. Set aside.
* Put rice in a bowl and beat in eggs. Place 1 rounded (heaped) tsp of mixture on the palm of your hand and flatten into a small circle. Top with a slice of ham, then a cube of cheese.
* Cover with another teaspoonful of rice, then gently roll mixture between your palms to make a neat ball. Repeat until ingredients are used up.
* Roll each ball in breadcrumbs to coat, then shake off excess and set aside.
* Heat sufficient oil for deep-frying over moderate heat; a small cube of stale bread dropped inside should turn golden in 40 seconds.
* Alternatively, preheat a deep-fryer to 190°C (375°F) and dip basket into hot oil before placing rice balls inside.
* Lower in balls, a few at a time, to cook. Fry for 5 minutes or until golden brown.
* Remove and drain on absorbent paper. Keep warm while cooking others.
* Serve as soon as last batch is drained.

venetian rice with peas and bacon

A classic Venetian dish of rice, peas and bacon, this recipe makes a great one-dish meal or a first course to an Italian meal. Use vegetable stock and omit the bacon for a vegetarian meal.

Serves 4–6

Ingredients

Olive oil	1 Tbsp
Lean bacon or ham	180 g (6 oz), chopped
Butter	60 g (2 oz)
Onion	1, peeled and thinly sliced
Shelled peas	450 g (1 lb)
Italian rice	450 g (1 lb), use Arborio or similar
Dry white wine	90 ml (3 fl oz / $^3/_8$ cup)
Vegetable or chicken stock	1.25 litres (2 pints / 5 cups), boiling hot
Salt	1 tsp or more to taste
Freshly ground black pepper	½ tsp or more to taste
Parmesan cheese	120 g (4 oz), grated

Method

- Heat oil in a large heavy saucepan over moderate heat. Add bacon or ham and fry, stirring occasionally, for 5 minutes or until crisp and golden brown. Remove with a slotted spoon and drain on absorbent paper.

- Add half the butter and melt over moderate heat. When foam subsides, add onion and cook, stirring occasionally, for 5–7 minutes or until onion is soft and translucent but not brown.

- Add peas and rice, reduce heat to low and cook, stirring frequently, for 5 minutes.

- Add wine and about one-third of stock. Regulate heat so that mixture is constantly bubbling. Stir occasionally with a fork.

- When rice swells and liquid has been absorbed, add another third of stock and regulate heat again. Repeat with remaining stock and rice should be tender and moist but still firm at the end.

- Stir in bacon, remaining butter, seasoning to taste and cheese. Mix well and simmer for 1 minute, stirring frequently.

- Remove from heat and dish out to serve. Add a sprinkle more of cracked black pepper, if desired.

stuffed courgettes

Easy to prepare, tasty and impressive-looking, this dish has hints of Middle Eastern flavours and makes either a substantial first course or a delightful light lunch.

Serves 4

Ingredients

Courgettes (zucchini)	4, large, trimmed and blanched
Minced beef	240 g (8 oz)
Chopped fresh dill	1 tsp, or ½ tsp dried
Chopped fresh marjoram	½ tsp, or ¼ tsp dried
Salt	½ tsp or to taste
Freshly ground black pepper	¼ tsp or to taste
Onion	1, finely chopped
Long-grain rice	2 Tbsp, washed, parboiled for 10 minutes and drained
Tomato juice	4 Tbsp
Butter	2 Tbsp
Tomato purée	1 Tbsp
Finely chopped basil leaves	2 tsp, or 1 tsp dried
Water	250 ml (8 fl oz / 1 cup)

Method

- Halve courgettes lengthways, then run the tip of a paring knife 0.5-cm ($^1/_4$-in) from the edge and all around. Use a teaspoon to scoop out flesh from each half and discard. Set courgette shells aside.

- Combine meat, dill, marjoram, seasoning to taste, onion and rice in a mixing bowl. Stir in 1 Tbsp tomato juice and mix well, then spoon into courgette shells.

- Melt half the butter in a large casserole over moderate heat. When foam subsides, remove from heat and arrange courgettes in a single layer on top, stuffing side up.

- Combine remaining tomato juice, tomato purée, basil and water in a small mixing bowl. Spoon mixture over courgettes.

- Cut remaining butter into 8 pieces and top each courgette half with one. Return casserole to moderate heat and bring to the boil.

- Cover casserole and reduce heat to low, then simmer for 30 minutes or until courgettes and rice are tender.

- Remove from heat and serve immediately.

pork congee

This congee has a delicate sweetness from the meat and scallop juices while the garnishing ingredients turn it into a richly textured and flavourful meal.

Ingredients

Minced pork	500 g (1 lb 1½ oz)
Light soy sauce	2 tsp or taste
Ground white pepper	1 tsp or taste
Sesame oil	½ tsp
Chinese cooking wine (*hua tiao*)	2 tsp
Corn flour (cornstarch)	1 tsp
Dried scallops	30 g (1 oz), soaked in 100 ml (3½ fl oz) water
Water	1.5 litres (48 fl oz / 6 cups)
Long-grain rice	200 g (7 oz), washed and drained

Garnishing

Crisp-fried shallots

Chopped spring onions (scallions)

Shredded ginger

Sliced red chillies (optional)

Light soy sauce

Ground white pepper

Sesame oil

Method

- Season pork with salt and pepper, then mix in sesame oil, wine and corn flour. Leave for 20 minutes, refrigerated.

- Meanwhile, steam scallops together with soaking liquid for 10–15 minutes or until soft. Shred scallops, reserve juices and set aside.

- Combine water and rice in a pot and bring to the boil. Reduce heat and simmer, partially covered, for 45 minutes or until rice is broken up and soft. Stir occasionally to prevent sticking.

- Shape pork into balls and lower into porridge to cook. When pork is cooked, add scallops and juices. Cook porridge for another 5 minutes, stirring occasionally.

- Ladle porridge into individual serving bowls. Top with desired amounts of each garnishing ingredient and serve.

briyani
(spiced rice with lamb)

A North Indian dish of Mogul origin, this is a fragrant mixture of meat, spices, nuts and saffron rice. Serve it alone with a yogurt salad or as part of a much larger and elaborate Indian meal, consisting of other meat and vegetable dishes with chutneys and pickles.

Serves 6

Ingredients

Ghee (clarified butter)	8 Tbsp, or cooking oil
Garlic	2 cloves, peeled and crushed
Ginger	2.5-cm (1-in), peeled and finely chopped
Cayenne pepper	¼ tsp
Cumin seeds	1½ tsp
Lean lamb	900 g (2 lb), cut into 2.5-cm (1-in) cubes
Cinnamon	1 stick, 10-cm (4-in) long
Cloves	10
Black peppercorns	8
Cardamom seeds	1 tsp
Yoghurt	300 ml (10 fl oz / 1¼ cups)
Salt	2 tsp
Water	2 litres (3⅕ pints / 8 cups)
Basmati rice	450 g (1 lb), washed, soaked in cold water for 30 minutes and drained
Saffron threads	½ tsp, soaked in 2 Tbsp boiling water for 10 minutes
Onions	2, peeled and thinly sliced
Almond slivers	45 g (1½ oz)
Pistachio nuts	45 g (1½ oz)
Raisins or sultanas	60 g (2 oz)

Method

- Heat half the ghee in a large pan over moderate heat. Add garlic, ginger, cayenne pepper and cumin seeds and fry for 3 minutes.

- Increase heat, add lamb and fry well for about 10 minutes or until meat is lightly browned on all sides.

- Stir in cinnamon, cloves, peppercorns, cardamom, yoghurt and 1 tsp salt. Mix well, then add 150 ml (5 fl oz) water and bring to the boil.

- Reduce heat, cover simmer for 35 minutes or until lamb is tender. Switch off heat.

- Bring remaining water to the boil in a large saucepan. Add remaining salt and drained rice. Boil briskly for 1½ minutes. Remove from heat, drain rice thoroughly and set aside.

- Grease a large ovenproof (flameproof) casserole with 1 Tbsp ghee, then spread one-third of parboiled rice over its base. Sprinkle over one-third of saffron solution.

- Remove half of lamb with a slotted spoon and spread out on top of rice. Add another one-third of rice sprinkled with saffron solution.

- Remove remaining lamb with a slotted spoon and place on top of second layer of rice. Finish with remaining rice, then pour lamb juices over evenly.

- Sprinkle on remaining saffron solution, then cover casserole with aluminium foil and seal, then place in a preheated oven at 180°C (350°F) for 20–30 minutes or until rice is cooked and has absorbed all the liquid.

- Meanwhile, heat remaining ghee in a small frying pan (skillet) over high heat. Add onions, reduce heat to moderate and fry, stirring frequently, for 10 minutes or until golden brown. Remove with a slotted spoon and drain on absorbent paper.

- Add almonds, pistachio nuts and raisins to pan, adding more ghee or oil, if necessary. Fry for 3 minutes or until nuts are lightly browned. Remove with a slotted spoon and set aside on a plate.

- Transfer rice to a large platter or individual serving plates. Top with fried nuts, raisins and onions and serve immediately with a chilled yoghurt salad, if desired.

austrian veal and rice casserole

This is a delicious casserole of veal and rice. It is quick, easy and economical to prepare and makes a very filling dish for the family. Serve it with a green salad.

Serves 4

Ingredients

Butter	60 g (2 oz)
Cooking oil	4 Tbsp
Boned veal shoulder	900 g (2 lb), cut into 2.5-cm (1-in) cubes
Onions	2, medium, peeled and finely chopped
Paprika	2 Tbsp
Chicken stock	625 ml (1 pint / 2½ cups)
White wine	4 Tbsp
Salt	1 tsp
Freshly ground black pepper	½ tsp
Dried thyme	1 tsp
Long-grain rice	300 g (10 oz), washed, soaked in water for 30 minutes and drained

Method

- Melt butter with oil in a large heatproof (flameproof) casserole over moderate heat.

- When foam subsides, add meat and onions. Fry, stirring frequently, for 5–8 minutes or until meat is browned.

- Add all remaining ingredients, except rice, and stir until well mixed. Bring to the boil, then reduce heat to low, cover casserole and simmer for 1¼ hours.

- Stir in rice, replace cover and simmer for 20–25 minutes or until rice is tender and has absorbed all the liquid.

- Remove from heat and serve as desired. Sprinkle over extra dried thyme for added aroma.

nasi goreng
(indonesian fried rice)

This is a splendid dish of rice with meat and prawns, and garnished in the traditional Indonesian manner.

Serves 4–6

Ingredients

Long-grain rice	360 g (12 oz), washed, soaked in water for 30 minutes and drained
Salt	2 tsp
Water	700 ml (23 fl oz/2¾ cups)
Cooking oil	4 Tbsp
Onions	2, medium, peeled and finely chopped
Red chillies	2, seeded and finely chopped, or ½ tsp hot chilli powder or more to taste
Dried prawn (shrimp) paste (*terasi* or *belacan*)	½ tsp
Garlic	1 clove, peeled and crushed
Ground coriander	2 tsp
Shelled prawns (shrimps)	180 g (6 oz)
Lamb or beef	180 g (6 oz), thinly sliced
Thick dark soy sauce	2 Tbsp
Brown sugar (optional)	2 tsp

Garnishing

Butter	1 Tbsp
Eggs	2, lightly beaten
Salt	¼ tsp
Cooking oil	2 Tbsp
Red chillies	2, thinly sliced
Onions	2, peeled and thinly sliced
Cucumber	½, peeled and diced
Spring onions (scallions)	6, cut into 2-cm (1-in) lengths

Method

- Combine rice, 1 tsp salt and water in a large saucepan. Bring to the boil over high heat, then cover, reduce heat to very low and simmer for 15 minutes or until rice is cooked. Remove from heat and set aside.

- Heat oil in another large saucepan over moderate heat. When oil is hot, reduce heat to moderate and fry onions, stirring occasionally, for 6–8 minutes or until golden brown.

- Add chillies or chilli powder, dried prawn paste, garlic and coriander. Fry for 5 minutes, stirring frequently.

- Stir in prawns and lamb or beef. Fry, stirring constantly, for 2–3 minutes or until ingredients are well mixed.

- Stir in cooked rice, dark soy sauce and remaining salt. Adjust seasoning to taste, adding sugar, if desired.

- When ingredients are well mixed, reduce heat to low and cook for about 10 minutes, stirring occasionally.

- Meanwhile, prepare garnishing ingredients. Melt butter in a frying pan (skillet) over moderate heat. When foam subsides, add eggs and salt. Cook, without stirring, for 1–2 minutes or until bottom of omelette is set and lightly browned.

- Turn omelette over and cook for another 1–2 minutes. Transfer omelette to a clean cutting board. Slice into 0.5-cm (¼-in) wide strips and set aside.

- Wipe frying pan with paper towels. Add oil and reheat over moderate–high heat. When oil is hot, reduce heat to moderate fry chillies for 2 minutes, stirring frequently.

- Add onions and fry, stirring occasionally, for 6–8 minutes or until golden brown. Remove from heat and set aside.

- When rice mixture is ready, transfer to a serving platter or divide among individual serving plates.

- Top with desired amounts of garnishing ingredients and serve.

chinese diced pork on crackling rice

A delicious and economical dish from China, it receives its unusual name from the distinctive crackling noise made by the rice when the pork sauce is poured over.

Serves 4

Ingredients

Lean pork fillets	450 g (1 lb), cut into 1-cm (½-in) cubes
Salt	1 tsp or to taste
Freshly ground black pepper	½ tsp or to taste
Corn flour (cornstarch)	1½ Tbsp
Cooked rice	450 g (1 lb)
Cooking oil for deep-frying	

Sauce

Chicken stock	150 ml (5 fl oz)
Light soy sauce	3 Tbsp
Sugar	1 Tbsp
Chinese cooking wine (*hua tiao*)	2 Tbsp, or dry sherry
Corn oil	2 Tbsp
Onion	1, peeled and thinly sliced
Garlic	1 clove, peeled and crushed
Corn flour (cornstarch)	1½ Tbsp, mixed with 4 Tbsp water

Method

- Season pork with salt and pepper, then sprinkle with corn flour and rub into meat with fingers. Set aside.

- Put rice in an ovenproof (flameproof) baking dish and place in a preheated oven at 140°C (275°F) for 15–20 minutes to dry out; rice should be slightly crisp.

- Meanwhile, heat sufficient oil for deep-frying in a deep pan over moderate heat. If using a deep-fryer, preheat to 180°C (350°F) and dip basket in hot oil before using.

- Deep-fry pork cubes, a few at a time, for 3–4 minutes or until golden brown. Drain pork on absorbent paper towels and maintain oil at 180°C (350°F).

- Prepare sauce. Combine stock, soy sauce, sugar and wine in a small bowl, beating with a fork until well blended. Set aside.

- Heat corn oil in a large frying pan (skillet) over moderate heat. Stir-fry onion and garlic for 1 minute, then add stock mixture and bring to the boil.

- Add pork and reduce heat to low. Baste well and simmer for 2 minutes or until sauce is hot, then add corn flour solution to thicken. Remove from heat and keep warm.

- Remove rice from oven and transfer to a narrow-meshed basket for deep-frying. Carefully lower basket into hot oil and cook for 1½ minutes, then drain on absorbent paper.

- Arrange rice on a serving dish and spoon sauce over. Serve immediately.

lamb and apricot pilaf

An exotic and relatively inexpensive dish, Lamb and Apricot Pilaf makes a delicious dinner party centrepiece. Serve with a tossed green salad and some crusty bread.

Serves 4

Ingredients

Butter	120 g (4 oz / ½ cup)
Onion	1, medium, peeled and thinly sliced
Boned leg of lamb	675 g (1½ lb), cut into 2.5-cm (1-in) cubes
Dried apricots	90 g (3 oz / ½ cup), soaked overnight, drained and halved
Raisins	3 Tbsp
Salt	2 tsp or to taste
Cinnamon	5-cm (2-in) stick, or ½ tsp ground
Freshly ground black pepper	¼ tsp or to taste
Water	1 litre (32 fl oz / 4 cups)
Long-grain rice	240 g (8 oz), washed, soaked in water for 30 minutes and drained

Method

- Melt butter in a large frying pan (skillet) over moderate heat. When foam subsides, add onion and cook, stirring occasionally, for 5 minutes or until soft and translucent but not brown.

- Add lamb and cook, stirring and turning occasionally, for 5–8 minutes or until lightly browned all over.

- Add apricots, raisins, 1 tsp salt, cinnamon, pepper and half the water. Bring to the boil, stirring occasionally.

- Reduce heat to low, cover pan and simmer for 1–1¼ hours or until meat is tender.

- Meanwhile, combine rice and remaining water and salt in a medium saucepan over high heat. Bring to the boil.

- Reduce heat to very low, cover and simmer for 15 minutes. If all the liquid has not been absorbed, continue to cook, uncovered, until rice is dry. Remove from heat.

- Spread one-third of rice over base of a medium ovenproof (flameproof) casserole, then top with half the meat mixture.

- Spread another third of rice on top and top with remaining meat mixture. Finish by covering meat with last third of rice.

- Cover casserole and bake in a preheated oven at 180°C (350°F) for 50 minutes or until rice is cooked through.

- Remove from oven, dish out and serve.

capsicums stuffed with lamb and rice

An adaptation of a Middle Eastern dish, Capsicums Stuffed with Lamb and Rice is delicious served with a green salad, lots of crusty bread and a robust red wine.

Serves 4

Ingredients

Red or green capsicums (bell peppers)	4, large
Cooking oil	1 Tbsp + 1 tsp
Onion	1, small, peeled and chopped
Garlic	1 clove, peeled and crushed
Minced lamb	240 g (8 oz)
Canned peeled tomatoes	420 g (14 oz)
Salt	1 tsp or to taste
Freshly ground black pepper	½ tsp or to taste
Coriander seeds	1 tsp, crushed
Cooked long-grain rice	150 g (5 oz)
Chopped mint leaves	1 tsp, or ½ tsp dried mint

Method

- Use a sharp knife to slice off about 2.5 cm (1 in) from tops of capsicums. Carefully remove seeds and pith, then set aside.
- Heat 1 Tbsp oil in a medium saucepan over moderate heat. Fry onion and garlic, stirring occasionally, for 5–7 minutes or until onion is soft and translucent.
- Add lamb and cook, stirring constantly, for 6–8 minutes or until well browned.
- Add tomatoes and can juices, seasoning to taste and coriander seeds. Cover saucepan, reduce heat to low and simmer for 30 minutes.
- Add rice and mint. Cook, stirring occasionally, for 5 minutes. Remove from heat.
- Grease a medium baking dish with 1 tsp oil. Fill capsicums with lamb mixture, then stand upright in baking dish.
- Place dish on centre shelf and bake in a preheated oven at 190°C (375°F) for 40 minutes or until capsicums are tender.
- Remove from oven and serve immediately. Garnish with extra mint leaves, if desired.

italian braised rice with bolognese sauce

A light Italian dish, this is a mixture of rice, Parma ham, meat-and-tomato-based sauce and Parmesan cheese.

Serves 4–6

Ingredients

Butter	120 g (4 oz)
Onion	1, medium, peeled and thinly sliced
Parma ham	120 g (4 oz), chopped
Italian rice	450 g (1 lb), use Arborio or similar
Dry white wine	90 ml (3 fl oz / 6 Tbsp)
Beef stock	1.25 litres (2 pints / 5 cups), boiling hot
Bolognese sauce	250 ml (8 fl oz / 1 cup)
Parmesan cheese	30 g (1 oz), grated

Garnishing

Grated Parmesan cheese
Cracked black pepper
Parsley

Method

- Melt 90 g (3 oz) butter in a large, heavy saucepan over moderate heat. When foam subsides, add onion and cook, stirring occasionally, for 5–7 minutes or until onion is soft and translucent but not brown.

- Add ham and rice, reduce heat to low and cook, stirring frequently, for 5 minutes.

- Add wine and about one-third of stock. Regulate heat so that mixture is constantly bubbling. Stir rice occasionally with a fork.

- When rice swells and all the liquid has been absorbed, add another third of stock and regulate heat again. Repeat with last third of stock; rice should be tender and moist but still firm at the end.

- Stir in remaining butter, Bolognese sauce and cheese. Simmer for 1 minute, stirring frequently.

- Remove from heat and divide among individual serving bowls. Garnish as desired and serve immediately.

italian braised saffron rice

One of the classic Italian first courses or accompaniments, this is a delicious mixture of rice, saffron, onion and Parmesan cheese.

Serves 4–6

Ingredients

Butter	4 Tbsp
Beef marrow	2 Tbsp, chopped
Onion	1, peeled and thinly sliced
Italian rice	450 g (1 lb), use Arborio or similar
Dry white wine	90 ml (3 fl oz)
Beef stock	1.25 litres (2 pints / 5 cups), boiling hot
Saffron threads	½ tsp, soaked in 1 Tbsp hot water
Parmesan cheese	60 g (2 oz), grated + extra for garnishing

Method

- Melt 3 Tbsp butter in a large, heavy saucepan over moderate heat.

- When foam subsides, add beef marrow and onion. Cook, stirring occasionally, for 5–7 minutes or until onion is soft and translucent but not brown.

- Add rice, reduce heat to low and cook for 5 minutes, stirring frequently.

- Add wine and about one-third of stock. Regulate heat so that mixture is constantly bubbling. Stir occasionally.

- When rice swells and all the liquid has been absorbed, add another third of stock and regulate heat again. Repeat with last third of stock; rice should be tender and moist but still firm at the end.

- Stir in saffron solution, remaining butter and cheese. Simmer for 1 minute, stirring frequently.

- Remove from heat and transfer to individual serving bowls. Garnish as desired and serve immediately.

middle eastern rice with meat and chick peas

This is a Middle Eastern-inspired dish and makes an interesting, delicious supper. Serve with salad of choice and lots of ice-cold beer.

Serves 4

Ingredients

Butter	120 g (4 oz)
Pickling (pearl) onions	12
Stewing steak	900 g (2 lb), cut into 2.5-cm (1-in) cubes
Chick peas	120 g (4 oz), soaked overnight and drained
Beef stock	250 ml (8 fl oz / 1 cup)
Salt	½ tsp or to taste
Freshly ground black pepper	½ tsp or to taste
Ground cumin	1 tsp
Ground turmeric	½ tsp
Long-grain rice	450 g (1 lb), washed, soaked in water for 30 minutes and drained

Method

• Melt butter in a large, heavy saucepan over moderate heat. When foam subsides, add onions and meat. Cook, stirring and turning, for 8–10 minutes or until onions are golden brown and meat is evenly browned.

• Add chick peas and stock, then top up with enough water to completely cover solid ingredients.

• Add seasoning to taste, cumin and turmeric. Stir to blend, cover saucepan and cook for 2 hours or until meat and chick peas are tender.

• Increase heat to moderate–high and bring to the boil. Stir in rice, cover and reduce heat to low. Simmer for 15–20 minutes or until rice is tender and all the liquid has been absorbed.

• Remove from heat and serve immediately.

desserts

nyonya sweet glutinous rice with custard

Scented with screwpine fragrance, this Nyonya (Straits Chinese) dessert makes a wonderful teatime snack or a great end to a spicy meal.

Ingredients

Glutinous rice	300 g (10 oz), washed and soaked in water for at least 4 hours, then drained
Coconut milk	250 ml (8 fl oz / 1 cup)
Salt	1 tsp
Screwpine (*pandan*) leaves	2, washed, bruised and knotted
Cooking oil for greasing	

Custard

Eggs	2
Sugar	60 g (2 oz)
Screwpine (*pandan*) essence (extract)	2–3 drops
Plain (all-purpose) flour	2 rounded (heaped) Tbsp, sifted
Salt	$1/4$ tsp
Coconut milk	150 ml (5 fl oz)
Green food colouring	2–3 drops

Method

- Combine glutinous rice, coconut milk and salt in a steaming tray; select a size so that rice is about 1.5-cm ($3/4$–in) high when spread out on tray.

- Place screwpine leaves on top and steam over rapidly boiling water for 15–20 minutes or until rice is cooked.

- Remove from steamer and discard screwpine leaves. Grease the back of a large spoon well and press down on rice to compress. Set aside to cool.

- Prepare custard. Beat eggs and sugar together until sugar is dissolved. Add all remaining ingredients and stir until mixture is smooth.

- Pour custard over glutinous rice and cover with a clean tea towel tautly pulled over; cloth must not touch custard. Steam over low heat for about 25 minutes or until custard is set.

- Remove from heat and cool before cutting to serve.

thai mango and sticky rice

This recipe is Thai-inspired and uses glutinous rice as a foil to enhance the complex taste and aroma of mangoes.

Ingredients

Glutinous rice	360 g (12 oz), soaked for at least 3 hours or overnight
Water	500 ml (16 fl oz / 2 cups)
Coconut milk	250 ml (8 fl oz / 1 cup)
Salt	1 tsp
Ripe mangoes	3, large, peeled, seeded and sliced

Coconut sauce

Coconut cream	250 ml (8 fl oz / 1 cup)
Screwpine (*pandan*) leaves	2, washed, bruised and knotted
Sugar	1 Tbsp
Salt	1 tsp

Method

- Drain rice and place in a rice cooker with water, coconut milk and salt. Cook until rice is tender. Cool thoroughly before using.

- Prepare sauce. Combine all ingredients in a saucepan and simmer, stirring constantly, until sugar is dissolved and sauce is slightly thickened.

- Spoon rice onto dessert plates and add mango slices. Spoon sauce over and serve.

indonesian black rice dessert

This dessert has an attractive dark aubergine colour and can be a filling way to end a meal or serve as hearty snack.

Ingredients

Black glutinous rice	400 g (14 oz)
Water	1.5 litres (48 fl oz / 6 cups)
Screwpine (*pandan*) leaves	2, knotted
Salt	1/4 tsp
Coconut milk	250 ml (8 fl oz / 1 cup)

Syrup

Palm sugar (*gula Melaka*)	50 g (2 oz), chopped
Water	125 ml (4 fl oz / 1/2 cup)

Method

- Rinse rice thoroughly and remove impurities. Soak in plenty of water for about 4 hours or preferably overnight.

- Drain rice and transfer to a large saucepan. Add 1.5 litres water and screwpine leaves. Simmer over medium heat for about 45 minutes or until tender but not mushy.

- Meanwhile, combine syrup ingredients in a small saucepan. Place over moderate–low heat and stir sugar is dissolved. Strain to remove impurities.

- When rice is tender, stir in syrup and salt. Adjust to taste with granulated sugar, if necessary.

- Remove from heat. Serve hot or at room temperature, topped with desired amount of coconut milk.

date and rice pudding

This creamy dessert has a delicate rose-like flavour. It must be cooked very slowly and stirred frequently to prevent the milk from burning.

Serves 4

Ingredients

Milk	1.25 litres (2 pints / 5 cups)
Rice	4 Tbsp
Sugar	5 Tbsp
Almond slivers	60 g (2 oz)
Dates	180 g (6 oz), pitted and chopped
Butter	2 Tbsp
Egg yolks	2
Rose water	2 tsp
Crystallised (candied) rose petals (optional)	

Method

- Combine milk and rice in a heavy, medium saucepan. Bring to the boil over moderate heat.
- Reduce heat to very low and simmer for 1–1½ hours, stirring frequently with a wooden spoon, or until consistency is that of thick cream.
- Add sugar, almonds and dates. Still stirring, bring to the simmer and cook mixture until it regains consistency of thick cream.
- Stir in butter and when it is well blended, remove from heat.
- Beat in egg yolks, one at a time. Stir in rose water. Pour pudding into a shallow dish or ramekins for individual servings. Leave to cool.
- Cover dish or ramekins with aluminium foil or cling film (plastic wrap) and refrigerate until chilled.
- Decorate with crystallised rose petals, if using, and serve.

apple and rice pudding

An inexpensive dessert, Apple and Rice Pudding looks attractive and has a pleasant sour-sweet taste. The quantity of sugar used depends on the tartness of the apples.

Serves 6

Ingredients

Long-grain rice	120 g (4 oz)
Milk	300 fl oz (10 fl oz / 1¼ cups), or milk mixed with single (light) cream
Lemon zest	grated from 1 lemon
Sugar	60 g (2 oz) + 6 Tbsp
Salt	a pinch
Eggs	2, yolks and whites separated
Apples	675 g (1½ lb), peeled and thinly sliced
Sultanas or raisins	60 g (2 oz)
Butter	2 Tbsp, cut into small cubes
Cider or apple juice	125 ml (4 fl oz / ½ cup)

Method

- Wash rice thoroughly, then soak in water for 30 minutes and drain before use.

- Combine milk, lemon zest, 60 g (2 oz) sugar and salt in a medium saucepan. Bring to the boil over moderate heat.

- Add rice and return to the boil, then reduce heat to very low. Cover and simmer for 10 minutes or until rice is cooked and milk has been absorbed. Remove from heat.

- Mix in egg yolks with a fork until well blended. Transfer half the mixture to a deep baking dish.

- Top with half the apples and sultanas. Sprinkle with 2 Tbsp sugar and dot with half the butter.

- Spread remaining rice over and top with remaining apples and sultanas. Sprinkle with another 2 Tbsp sugar and dot with remaining butter.

- Pour cider or apple juice over and bake for 45 minutes in a preheated oven at 180°C (350°F). Remove pudding from oven and reset oven to 150°C (300°F).

- Beat egg whites until stiff, then fold in 2 Tbsp sugar. Spread meringue over top of pudding, then bake for 20 minutes or until top is golden brown.

- Leave to cool slightly, then cut and serve.

risalamande
(danish rice and almond dessert)

Delectable and easy to make, this Danish dessert has a French origin and may be served with a jam sauce.

Serves 6

Ingredients

Sugar	3 Tbsp
Milk	660 ml (22 fl oz / 2¾ cups)
Long-grain rice	240 g (8 oz), washed, soaked in water for 30 minutes and drained
Double (heavy) cream	300 ml (10 fl oz / 1¼ cups)
Vanilla essence (extract)	1 tsp
Almonds slivers	3 Tbsp

Method

- Combine sugar and milk in a heavy, medium saucepan. Bring to the boil over moderate heat. Stir frequently until sugar is dissolved.

- Add rice and return to the boil, stirring constantly.

- Reduce heat to very low, cover and simmer for about 15 minutes or until rice is tender and milk has been absorbed. Stir occasionally.

- Remove from heat and set aside to cool completely.

- Meanwhile, put cream into a small mixing bowl and beat with a wire whisk or rotary beater until thick but not stiff.

- Fold cream, vanilla essence and almonds into cold rice. Mix thoroughly.

- Spoon mixture into a glass serving bowl or ramekins for individual servings. Refrigerate for at least 1 hour before serving.

- Spoon some jam sauce of choice over and top with a blanched almond over each serving, if desired.

empress rice pudding

One of the classic French desserts, this is a marvellous mixture of rice, crème de vanille, kirsch and candied fruit. It is very rich and makes a spectacular end to a formal party.

Serves 6

Ingredients

Butter	1 Tbsp
Short-grain rice	90 g (3 oz)
Sugar	60 g (2 oz)
Milk	950 ml (1½ pints / 3¾ cups) milk
Vanilla essence (extract)	1½ tsp
Candied peel	2 Tbsp
Glacé (candied) cherries	2 Tbsp
Kirsch (cherry brandy)	2 Tbsp
Egg yolks	3
Gelatine	30 g (1 oz), dissolved in 6 Tbsp hot water
Crème de vanille (vanilla-flavoured crème liqueur)	240 ml (8 fl oz), chilled
Double (heavy) cream	300 ml (10 fl oz / 1¼ cups), beaten until stiff
Apricot jam	2 Tbsp

Method

- Grease a 1.25-litre (2-pint / 5-cup) baking dish with butter. Add rice, sugar, milk and vanilla essence and stir to mix.

- Bake in a preheated oven at 150°C (300°F) for 3 hours.

- Meanwhile, mix together candied peel, glacé cherries and kirsch in a small bowl. Set aside to marinate at room temperature.

- Remove baking dish from oven and beat in egg yolks, one at a time, then beat in gelatine solution. Set aside to cool for 15 minutes.

- Beat in fruit and kirsch mixture. Fold in crème de vanille and cream with a metal spoon. Set aside.

- Lightly coat interior of a 1.25-litre (2-pint / 5-cup) mould with apricot jam. Alternatively, use smaller moulds of desired shape for individual servings.

- Pour rice mixture into greased mould and smoothen surface with the back of a wooden spoon.

- Refrigerate for 2 hours or until mixture has set, then remove and dip bottom of mould quickly into hot water.

- Invert a serving dish and cover mould, then turn over so rice mixture can slide out.

- Decorate, if desired, with extra candied peel and almond slivers. Serve immediately.

riz melba
(rice and peach dessert)

This is a simple-to-make and delectable dessert, which tastes equally good served on its own or with Chantilly cream—beat 250 ml (8 fl oz / 1 cup) chilled whipping cream until thick, add 2 Tbsp icing (confectioner's) sugar and 1/2 tsp vanilla essence (extract), then continue beating until peaks form.

Serves 4

Ingredients

Sugar	60 g (2 oz)
Milk	625 ml (1 pint / 2½ cups)
Short-grain rice	180 g (6 oz)
Egg yolk	1
Fresh peaches	2, blanched, peeled, halved and pitted, or canned peaches
Raspberry jam	120 g (4 oz)
Double (heavy) cream	2 Tbsp
Almond slivers	60 g (2 oz), lightly toasted

Syrup

Sugar	120 g (4 oz / ½ cup)
Water	120 ml (4 fl oz / ½ cup)

Method

- Combine sugar, milk and rice in a medium saucepan. Place over moderate heat and bring to the boil, stirring constantly.
- Reduce heat to low, cover and simmer for 30–35 minutes or until rice is tender and milk has been absorbed.
- Stir in egg yolk, then remove from heat and set aside to cool completely.
- Meanwhile, prepare syrup. Combine both ingredients in a medium saucepan. Cook over moderate heat until sugar is dissolved, stirring constantly.
- Increase heat to moderate–high and allow syrup to boil for 4 minutes, without stirring.
- Reduce heat to low and add peach halves, cut sides down and in one layer. Poach for 3–4 minutes or until tender but still retaining shape. Remove with a slotted spoon and leave to cool.
- Stir jam into syrup and cook for 2 minutes, stirring constantly. When sauce is smooth, remove from heat and set aside to cool.
- Stir cream into cooled rice, then divide among 4 individual serving cups. Spoon syrup over and top each glass with one peach half.
- Sprinkle flaked almonds over and refrigerate for 1 hour before serving.

zarda
(sweet pilaf)

Sweet Pilaf is is served all over Pakistan and India during Muslim festivals and feasts.

Serves 6

Ingredients

Butter	3 Tbsp
Long-grain rice	360 g (12 oz), washed, soaked in water for 30 minutes and drained
Salt	1/4 tsp
Cardamoms	6 pods, coarsely crushed
Cinnamon	5-cm (2-in) stick, crushed
Milk	625 ml (1 pint / 2 1/2 cups)
Sugar	2–4 Tbsp, to taste
Double (heavy) cream	4 Tbsp
Saffron threads	1/2 tsp, soaked in 2 Tbsp hot milk for 20 minutes
Lemon juice	2 tsp

Decoration

Blanched almonds	15
Blanched pistachio nuts	4 Tbsp, chopped
Raisins	6 Tbsp

Method

- Melt butter in a large ovenproof (flameproof) casserole over moderate heat. When foam subsides, add rice, salt, cardamoms and cinnamon. Fry for 5 minutes, stirring frequently.

- Stir in milk and sugar to taste. When sugar has dissolved, bring mixture to the boil, then reduce heat to very low.

- Cover casserole and simmer for 15–20 minutes or until rice is cooked and all the milk has been absorbed.

- Stir in cream, saffron solution and lemon juice. Replace cover and simmer for a further 5 minutes.

- Transfer casserole to a preheated oven at 150°C (300°F) and cook for 10 minutes. Remove from oven.

- Spoon rice onto a platter or individual serving plates. Decorate as desired and serve immediately.

glossary

1. Arborio rice

Arborio rice grains are medium length and roundish. It is an ideal risotto rice because the grains become creamy but never mushy even with prolonged cooking. Arborio rice is named after a town in Italy. Situated in Po valley, Arborio, the town became famous for growing these grains.

2. Basmati rice

Basmati rice grains are long and and increase considerably in length when cooked. They require slightly more water than Thai or Japanese rices to cook and cooked basmati is dry and fluffy, as well as deeply aromatic. Basmati rice figures prominently in Indian cuisine, and brown and white varieties of basmati are sold. Brown basmati, although less common, has a stronger flavour. Like other types of brown rice, however, brown basmati contains more fibre.

3. Black glutinous rice

Also known as black sticky rice or simply as black rice to some, black glutinous rice is most popularly used in a soupy dessert in Southeast Asia that is eaten with coconut milk or cream. Despite its name, black glutinous rice takes on a deep aubergine colour when cooked.

4. Chinese five-spice powder

A seasoning that is made from Sichuan (Szechuan) peppercorns, star anise, cloves, cinnamon and fennel seeds, Chinese five-spice powder is a versatile ingredient. It can be used as part of a marinade, added during cooking or served at the table as a dip. Roast duck is one dish that involves five-spice powder as a dipping condiment.

5. Crisp-fried shallots

Sold ready-made in supermarkets and Asian stores, crisp-fried shallots are deeply aromatic and intensely flavourful. In the past, cooks used to thinly sliced shallots and then deep-fry them over low heat until dark brown and crisp. The oil that was used to fry the shallots, known as shallot oil, is also reused. In a Chinese household, shallot oil is typically drizzled over rice congee, together with a few drops of sesame oil, for added flavour.

6. Dried prawn (shrimp) paste (*belacan*)

Extremely pungent, dried prawn paste is generally known as *belacan* to Malay-speakers and *terasi* to Indonesians. Always used in fairly small quantities, it adds a complex salty flavour to the dish, and its pungency transforms into an inviting aroma with cooking.

7. Dried prawns (shrimps) (*hae be*)

Although tiny in size, dried prawns pack a punch in terms of flavour when cooked. A handy store-cupboard item, dried prawns keep safely for up to a year if stored in an airtight container and refrigerated.

8. Dried scallops
Chiefly used in Chinese cooking, dried scallops are useful for making flavourful stocks in a flash. Simply boil them up in some water for a clear stock, and reserve both stock and scallops, which would have disintegrated into shreds, for cooking. Boiled scallop shreds are chewy, somewhat like cuttlefish and add great texture to a green leafy stir-fry or congee.

8.

9. Dried shiitake mushrooms
Also known as black Chinese mushrooms, dried shiitake mushrooms have a deep earthy flavour that may be too pungent for some palates. These mushrooms require soaking to soften before use, and the stems are usually snipped off because they can be quite tough even after prolonged cooking.

10. Fresh shiitake mushrooms
Fresh shiitake mushrooms are considerably milder in flavour than their dried cousins. With caps that are about 5-cm (2-in) in diameter, these fresh mushrooms can make a chunky and filling meal. Their milder flavour also allows them to blend better in a dish by taking on the dominant flavour.

9. **10.**

11. Glutinous rice
Also known as sticky rice, glutinous rice has medium grains that are a more opaque white than other types of white rice. It becomes very sticky when cooked, and it is common in Asian cooking, appearing in main dishes and desserts alike. Although it is known as Japanese rice to some, it is ill advised to use glutinous rice to prepare sushi as it is simply too sticky. Trying to spread cooked glutinous rice on a nori (seaweed) sheet will most likely cause tears.

12. Japanese (calrose) rice
Short-grain rice generally turns out more moist and sticky than long-grain varieties. This is true of Japanese rice, also known as calrose rice. When cooked, Japanese rice grains tend to clump together when fluffed up with a pair of chopsticks but are not impossible to separate like glutinous rice. It is this semi-sticky quality that makes it ideal for making sushi. The U.S. and Australia are leading producers of calrose rice.

11. **12.**

13. Japanese seven-spice seasoning
Nanami or shichimi togarashi is a seasoning mainly made from sansho pepper, dried mandarin peel, nori shreds and poppy and sesame seeds. The ingredients used in the bottled blend varies slightly from maker to maker. Slightly spicy, the seasoning gives a lift to soups, noodles or stir-fries with a few shakes.

14. Kaffir lime leaves
Known to Malay-speakers as *daun limau purut*, kaffir lime leaves are popular with Southeast Asian cooks, especially Thai ones. Shredded and added to a dish, the leaves impart an inimitable zest and herby taste. They are also known as "double lime leaves" because of how the leaves grow in pairs.

13. **14.**

15. Long brown rice

Also known as wholegrain rice, brown rice in general has a reputation for being more healthful but also less tasty than long white rice. The coloured outer layer of brown rice contains bran and germ, which, in turn, contain the extra fibre, making it chewy and more nutritious. Because of the extra layer that was not milled off, as is the case with white rice, long brown rice does not turn out as tender or as fluffy as its white counterpart when cooked.

15.

16. Pickling onions

Native to southwestern Asia, the onion plant is a part of the lily family and it is cultivated for its edible bulb. Many types of onions, whether red, yellow, white, large or small, are seen in markets around the world today. Pickling onions, in particular, are white and bite-size. Usually no larger than a golf ball, they are sometimes also known as pearl onions.

17. Pork floss

Pork floss refers to tougher cuts of the meat that have been cooked and then dehydrated to a point where the final product resembles coarse cotton. Traditionally, the meat would have been cooked in a sweet soy-based mixture until the muscle fibres break down, and then dried—first in an oven, then in a dry wok—until light and fluffy. A popular condiment with Chinese cooks, pork floss is used as a flavourful topping for congee and filling for pastries, as well as a snack favoured especially by children for its sweet taste. Pork floss is quite expensive not only because it is labour intensive to produce, but also because only 1 kg (2 lb 3 oz) of floss is made from 5 kg (10 lb 15 oz) of meat. Chicken and fish can also be made into floss.

18. Saffron threads

Saffron is one of the most expensive spices in the world, with Spain and Iran being leading producers. The saffron plant belongs to the iris family and saffron threads are really the stigmas of the plant. Saffron threads are richly fragrant when cooked and the aroma that rises from just a pinch is remarkable. Saffron threads also give the dish hues of red, orange and yellow.

19. Salted fish

Salted fish is a flavouring agent often used in Asian cooking. It comes in many grades and varieties and can smell pungent to some before and while it is cooked. Shown in the picture is salted threadfin or *ikan kurau* to Malay-speakers. Salted threadfin is generally regarded as superior to the generic salted fish found in Asian markets. Salted threadfin has a finer texture and a more complex salty taste that does well in enhancing the flavours of the dish to which it has been added. Salted fish is often also crisp-fried and pounded for a flavourful, sprinkling garnish. Always rinse salted fish of excess salt before use.

16.

17.

18.

19.

20. Screwpine (*pandan*) leaves

Better known as *pandan* leaves, screwpine leaves impart a subtle but irresistible fragrance when cooked. However, they cannot be ingested and should be discarded before serving. To use, wash, drain and knot leaves together before adding to the pot. Some cooks prefer to shred the leaves lengthways before knotting for a stronger aroma.

21. Short brown rice

The short varieties of rice are generally more sticky than their longer counterparts when cooked. Between brown and white short rice varieties, however, the brown variety does not turn out as sticky as the white variety. Furthermore, all brown rice varieties require longer cooking times than their white counterparts, almost twice as long. Brown rice varieties also have a shorter shelf life. Store brown rice in a cool, dark place for no more than three months.

22. Sweet short rice

Also known as mochi rice, sweet short rice grains are short and become sticky when cooked. Although sweet rice is sweeter than regular rice, the sweetness is extremely subtle. The rice is sticky because of its high starch content. This rice appears prominently in Japanese cuisine.

23. Thai brown jasmine rice

The unpolished version of Thai jasmine rice is a fairly recent addition to rice eating traditions in Asia. Arguably brought about by the movement for a healthier diet and lifestyle at the turn of the twenty-first century, the rice is sometimes also known as red jasmine rice.

24. Thai jasmine rice

Also known as Thai fragrant rice, jasmine rice grown in Thailand is subtly but distinctively aromatic. Although it is also considered a long-grain rice, it requires less cooking than basmati and is also more moist when cooked. Jasmine rice is popular in Southeast Asia.

25. Turmeric

Turmeric is also known as "yellow ginger", and it is not hard to see why. Underneath the rhizome's brown peel is a bright orange and yellow flesh. When pounded to a pulp and squeezed, the resulting turmeric juice can make the dish to which it has been added bright yellow. In fact, it also stains any surface it comes into contact with, and the marks are difficult to remove.

26. Wild rice

Also known as Indian rice, wild rice are grass seeds from an aquatic plant related to the rice family. Although wild rice is not categorically a rice, it is used in much the same way. Wild rice is also more flavourful than rice, chewier in terms of texture and contains more protein and nutrients. Probably the only disadvantage wild rice has against generic rice is its high price.

Weights and Measures

Quantities for this book are given in Metric, Imperial and American (spoon and cup) measures. Standard spoon and cup measurements used are: 1 tsp = 5 ml, 1 Tbsp = 15 ml, 1 cup = 250 ml. All measures are level unless otherwise stated.

Liquid And Volume Measures

Metric	Imperial	American
5 ml	1/6 fl oz	1 teaspoon
10 ml	1/3 fl oz	1 dessertspoon
15 ml	1/2 fl oz	1 tablespoon
60 ml	2 fl oz	1/4 cup (4 tablespoons)
85 ml	2 1/2 fl oz	1/3 cup
90 ml	3 fl oz	3/8 cup (6 tablespoons)
125 ml	4 fl oz	1/2 cup
180 ml	6 fl oz	3/4 cup
250 ml	8 fl oz	1 cup
300 ml	10 fl oz (1/2 pint)	1 1/4 cups
375 ml	12 fl oz	1 1/2 cups
435 ml	14 fl oz	1 3/4 cups
500 ml	16 fl oz	2 cups
625 ml	20 fl oz (1 pint)	2 1/2 cups
750 ml	24 fl oz (1 1/5 pints)	3 cups
1 litre	32 fl oz (1 3/5 pints)	4 cups
1.25 litres	40 fl oz (2 pints)	5 cups
1.5 litres	48 fl oz (2 2/5 pints)	6 cups
2.5 litres	80 fl oz (4 pints)	10 cups

Dry Measures

Metric	Imperial
30 grams	1 ounce
45 grams	1 1/2 ounces
55 grams	2 ounces
70 grams	2 1/2 ounces
85 grams	3 ounces
100 grams	3 1/2 ounces
110 grams	4 ounces
125 grams	4 1/2 ounces
140 grams	5 ounces
280 grams	10 ounces
450 grams	16 ounces (1 pound)
500 grams	1 pound, 1 1/2 ounces
700 grams	1 1/2 pounds
800 grams	1 3/4 pounds
1 kilogram	2 pounds, 3 ounces
1.5 kilograms	3 pounds, 4 1/2 ounces
2 kilograms	4 pounds, 6 ounces

Length

Metric	Imperial
0.5 cm	1/4 inch
1 cm	1/2 inch
1.5 cm	3/4 inch
2.5 cm	1 inch

Oven Temperature

	°C	°F	Gas Regulo
Very slow	120	250	1
Slow	150	300	2
Moderately slow	160	325	3
Moderate	180	350	4
Moderately hot	190/200	375/400	5/6
Hot	210/220	410/425	6/7
Very hot	230	450	8
Super hot	250/290	475/550	9/10

Abbreviation

tsp	teaspoon
Tbsp	tablespoon
g	gram
kg	kilogram
ml	millilitre